Mosaik

Haruyo Kataoka/Friederun Köhnen

JAPAN

A Cookbook

– The Flavour of Zen –

Mosaik

Special thanks to

Kyoto, Immermannstrasse, Düsseldorf and their helpful staff for the loan of
Japanese equipment, the beautiful tableware, and all the other
kitchen utensils.

Gerhard Bönig for help with the photography.
And to the Mauritius photo agency for the picture of Mount Fujiyama
on pages 2/3.

The Food Professionals/Köhnen
Concept and advice: Haruya Kataoka
Original text: Jutta A. Jacobs
Translation of recipes: Kazuko Yamaguchi
English translation and adaptation:
UPS Translations, London (Paul Fletcher, Tom Wesel)
Typesetting: The Printed Word, London
Recipes prepared by The Food Professionals/Versuchsküche
Photos: Ulrike Breu
Food stylist: Christa Schraa
Layout: Ina Hochbach

Published by Mosaik Books a division of GeoCenter International U.K. Limited

© Original edition: 1990 Mosaik Verlag GmbH, Munich 5 4 3 2 1
© English language edition: 1993 Mosaik Verlag GmbH, Munich 5 4 3 2 1

Origination by Arti Litho, Trento
Printed at Mohndruck Graphische Betriebe GmbH, Gütersloh
Printed in Germany
ISBN 3-576-80018-2

CONTENTS

6

COOKING THE JAPANESE WAY –
A FEAST FOR THE EYES
AND A TREAT FOR THE TASTE-BUDS

Many people believe that Japanese food consists of tiny morsels of raw fish and that the most important thing is to present it in an attractive way.
That may be true to some extent.
A Japanese meal consists of several small, carefully prepared portions, served at intervals. Of course, there may well be some small pieces of raw fish to enjoy, but they are by no means all that there is to look forward to at a Japanese table.
The choice and combination of individual ingredients, the manner in which they are served and the beautiful garnishes are always in harmony with the season.
A Japanese menu is sensitive to the moods of Spring, Summer, Autumn and Winter.

Before venturing into the Japanese kitchen, there is a story to be told:
It is springtime, cherry blossom time. The Cherry Blossom Festival will be starting soon. Fumi Morimoto has invited three of her close friends round for a meal.
The days are mild, the countryside is bathed in a soft light and the cherry blossom is already out in Fumi's garden. Her husband planted a small tree a few years earlier.
But the day is young, the sun has only just risen and Fumi is not concerned about the garden. There will be plenty of time for that later.
She gets dressed and sets off for the market in the small town where she lives with her family. It is close to the sea and there are plenty of delicious fresh foods on offer.
She walks up and down past the stalls a couple of times, but she soon makes up her mind. She is going to buy some fresh

fish, tender young vegetables, carefully packaged, fresh shiitake mushrooms, young bamboo shoots and a few ready-made mochi cakes.
To this she adds a small bunch of young, beautiful, pale-green leaves, a sprig of flower buds and sake.
After her shopping trip, Fumi goes into her small kitchen and prepares a salad, using bamboo shoots, perfect for the springtime. All her other household chores are performed with one aim in mind – to enable her guests to enjoy their meal as much as possible.
As the sun moves slowly across the sky, Fumi begins to make further preparations. First she sweeps the garden with a birch broom, clearing away any leaf or twig that is in the wrong place or a scrap of paper that may have blown in. The small cherry tree also needs a little attention. There's a branch that upsets the equilibrium and it will have to be pruned. Now everything is to her satisfaction. The pebbles look immaculate, the tree sways gently in the breeze. The intricately designed stream flowing through the garden babbles contentedly, reflecting Fumi's feelings as her thoughts turn once again to the preparations for her guests.
Inside there are still a few things to do. Fumi lovingly decorates the table with the leaves and the sprig of flower buds. Could the arrangement possibly mirror the small cherry tree outside in the garden? Then there is the arrangement three white pebbles and an oval bowl filled with fresh water standing by the door from the small garden into the dining-room.
Now Fumi has a quick look through her tableware and checks to see that it is in

keeping with the springtime meal she has planned. Each course requires a different type of service – attractive earthenware bowls, translucent porcelain or a bamboo basket. The blossoming cherry tree is the focal point of tonight's meal. The bowls and plates must harmonise with this theme, porcelain plates with a cherry blossom pattern for the bamboo shoot salad, a red-lacquered fish plate and some small branches of cherry blossom on which to rest the chopsticks.

Soon the guests will be arriving and it is time for Fumi to start preparing the soup. It is a simple, yet subtly-flavoured consommé with two or three pieces of fresh vegetables cut into little stars floating on top. The fish also needs to be prepared. Up until now, it has been resting on ice, but is not frozen. Fumi guts it and then washes it carefully. It is filleted, thinly sliced and arranged attractively on the dish. Perhaps she will lay a small leaf on top to represent a bird which was singing in her garden earlier that day. Fumi uses the shiitake mushrooms to prepare a little appetiser which both looks and tastes good. The ready-made cakes are wrapped in cherry leaves which have been blanched for a few seconds.

The guests are here. Fumi's husband has picked them up on his way home from work. As the householder, he is expected to greet the guests on the doorstep, so he has hurried on ahead. Each guest is offered a small cloth dipped in hot water with which to wipe his or her hands. This helps to refresh and relax everyone and sets the mood.

Fumi invites them to the table. She brings warm sake and pours a drop in a small bowl for each guest, her husband and herself. The guests admire Fumi's floral arrangement. She is delighted that they immediately notice and comment on the beauty of her small garden.

The visitors enjoy the meal and all of them are full of praise for the quality of the food and the freshness of the ingredients.

By the time the guests have gone, the sun has set and Fumi's garden basks in the gentle light of a Japanese lantern.

That was a short story about a Japanese supper. Let it inspire you. Perhaps now you will understand why not every recipe in this book serves four people.

If you have read the introduction to each chapter and have had a good look through the whole book, you will see that we have tried to keep to the Japanese notion of harmony. You will have to search hard to find out how to prepare the sesame seeds referred to in the chapter on meat. That is because the relevant information is to be found in the chapter on herbs and spices. Too complicated? We don't think so, since the book was designed with easy reference in mind. But anyway, part of the pleasure of reading is getting to know a book well!

EQUIPMENT

Bamboo mats are used for rolling up sushi. They are about 20 cm/8 inches wide and 30 cm/12 inches long.

Bamboo skewers. Small skewers made from bamboo, sometimes in their natural colour or sometimes coloured green. They are usually used for holding ingredients together.

Bowls. Almost any type of bowl is used – large, small, expensive, cheap, delicate or crude, bowls made from the finest china, beautifully lacquered bowls or rough clay pottery. In winter, hand-thrown pottery is preferred, in summer, cooler porcelain. Sake bowls are usually small and have a small base. Then there are tiny bowls for spices, special bowls for soy sauce, bigger bowls for rice, various types of bowls for tea, depending on the occasion and time of year, bowls for cakes and bowls for sweets. For soups, lacquered bowls with lids are normally used. Some bowls are for use only with meat dishes, some are just for fish. There are simply so many different types it is not possible to mention them all here.

Chopsticks are used every day. There are the larger, round ones for cooking, long ones for stirring or for *Shabushabu*. Chopsticks for eating with are usually natural wood with decorative inscriptions or they may be lacquered. Women, with their smaller hands, often prefer to use shorter chopsticks than the men.

Frying-pans: There are square or rectangular pans with raised sides for cooking thick omelettes. There are flat, round or oval pans for wafer-thin omelettes. For frying fish and vegetables, a cast iron pan is the best choice.

Graters are made of metal and are used for grating radish, ginger and other roots. They are also used for *Momiji-oroshi.*

Grills. When the Japanese talk about grilling, they usually mean a charcoal grill, but electric grills are also used.

Hot stones. These are not just any stones, but smooth, attractively-shaped ones. The Japanese use stones which they have found, but don't be tempted to follow their example. You can buy special cooking stones with handles, for use as a hot plates.

Knives

In Japanese cooking, all knives must have extremely sharp blades and should always be kept in good condition. Sometimes the blades are decorated with engravings.

Fish knives are large and pointed. They are generally used for preparing sashimi and for filleting fish.

Sushi knives are long, narrow and with a straight lower edge. They are marvellous for cutting any ingredient, but are especially good for cutting exact lengths of rolled sushi.

Vegetable knives are large and wide with a straight lower edge. They cut vegetables cleanly without flattening them.

Lacquered tableware is a subject of interest and deserves a special mention. Whether it is a small, lacquered tray or a red bowl with a lid for soup – lacquerware is very fragile. In the drier areas of Japan, the lacquer can easily flake off. Items of lacquerware should always be stored in a cupboard with a glass of water and are certainly not suitable for the dishwasher. After use they should be rinsed in warm water with just a drop of washing-up liquid and then dried with a soft cloth.

Leaves are greatly valued, simply for serving or for decoration. Larger leaves, such as lotus leaves, are used instead of plates or as a tray.

Pestle and Mortar. A special mortar is used for crushing sesame seeds. It has a wide, open bowl which has a roughened inside surface.

Moulds for vegetables, fruit and sweets. The Japanese love natural shapes. Fruit, vegetables and sweets are often cut into the shape of flowers or leaves.

Plates. Like trays, these come in all sorts of different shapes and sizes.

Platters are used for preparation or serving. They come in all shapes and sizes. Some look like trays and others look like bowls.

Portable hot plates can be very useful in a Japanese kitchen, as so many dishes are prepared at the table or at least need to be kept warm there.

Chopstick rests. These can be made from virtually anything and come in all shapes and sizes. A small sprig of cherry blossom or a length of bamboo cane, perhaps a tiny porcelain stand in the shape of a leaf – all these are commonly used. Sometimes a piece of folded paper is all that is necessary.

Rice spoons are about the size of a side plate and carved from wood.

Sake bowls should be used for Japanese rice wine. Special bottles are used for warming the sake. These are left to stand in warm water and then the wine is poured into the special bowls.

Steamers are special pots made from cast-iron. They are used to prepare dishes which need to be gently steamed. A Japanese steamer consists of two pots, one on top of the other. The upper pot has a perforated base and fits exactly over the lower pot, like a double-boiler. The water is boiled in the lower pot and ingredients are cooked in the upper pot. Another type of steamer is a large flat wooden tub also with a perforated base. It is made from woven bamboo and is placed over a small pot containing boiling water. The ingredients cook gently in the upper half.

Trays come in various shapes and types. There are black lacquered trays, simple wooden trays, trays made from porcelain. Although generally used for serving, they may also be used for preparing dishes.

Wooden tub. A large container made of unlacquered and untreated wood, which has been designed specially for preparing sushi rice. The Japanese call it a *hangiri*. It is not an essential piece of equipment and a small wooden box or a wooden tray makes a good substitute. Rice cooked in one of these tubs is always a success, because the wood absorbs the excess moisture from the rice. They will take on a polished look if repeatedly shaken and fanned.

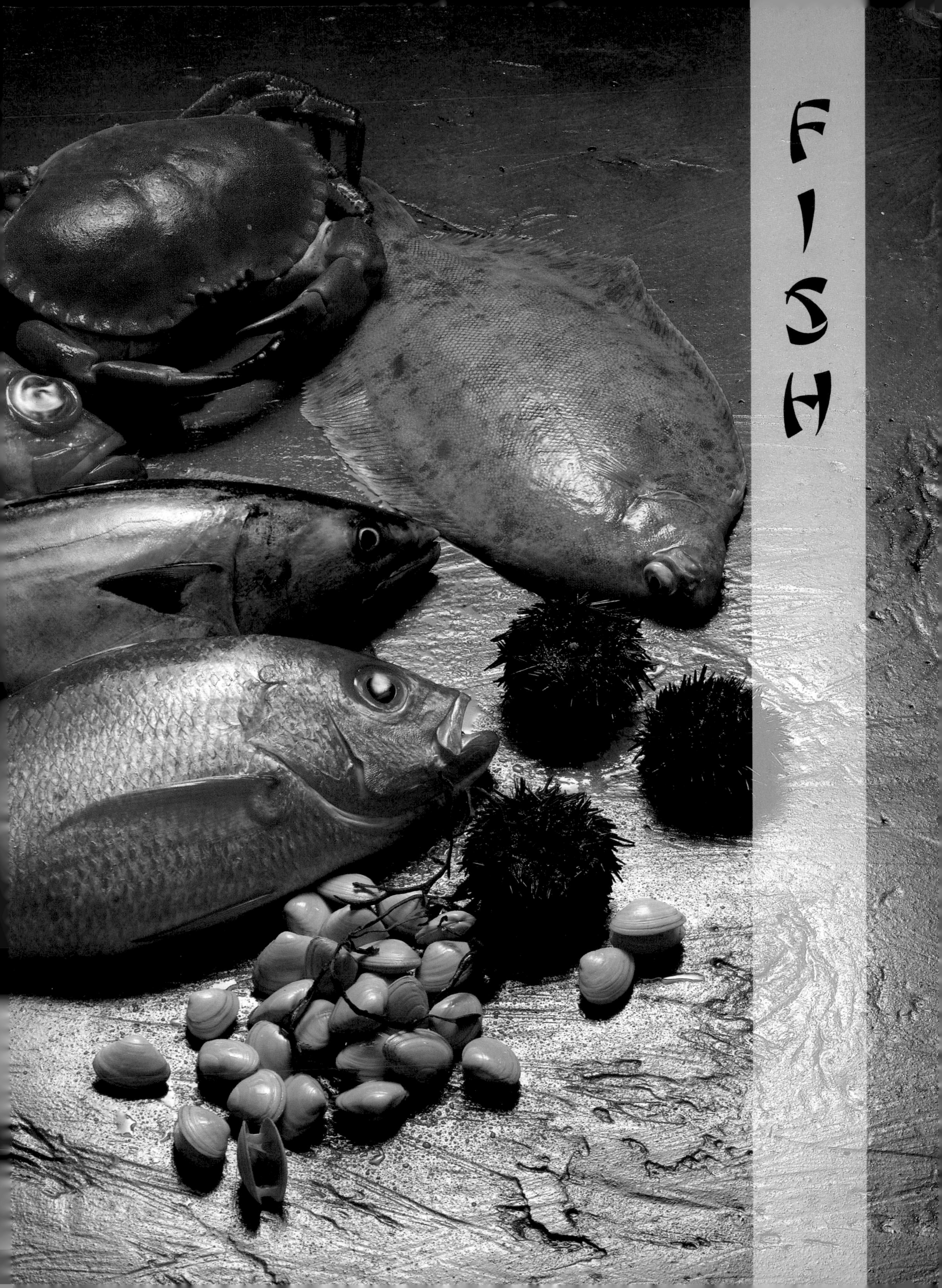

FISH

FISH AND SEAFOOD

Fresh Fish Daily

A Japanese kitchen without fish or seafood is hard to imagine.

There is fish all the year round and for every meal. It is eaten in a wide variety of ways – raw, steamed or baked, in sauces or in stews. Sometimes shrimps are eaten in their shells and sea-urchin roe are used to make a sauce to eat with squid.

The most important thing for the Japanese is the freshness and quality of the fish and seafood. They have a horror of pre-packed deep-frozen plaice or marinated mussels from a jar. It is not only quality that counts, but also the need for special care in preparation. One example of that is *sashimi*. In Japan, this apparently simple recipe is reserved for the Itamae, literally 'the man at the chopping board'. The cook who is able to prepare sashimi is held in the highest esteem. A blunt knife or a wrong move can ruin this delicate fish dish.

What to look for at the fish counter

As soon as a fish is dead, it will start to decay. Real freshness is only there in life. The Japanese believe that fish must be eaten as soon as possible. Top quality fish can only be fresh fish. A really fresh fish has absolutely no smell.
Some points to look out for:
– bright, round eyes, which protrude slightly. If the eyes are sunken and lack sparkle, the fish is no longer fresh.
– moist gills, with a bright red colouring.
– shiny, silvery, moist scales.
– fresh fish smell faintly of the sea.
Fish keep better if they are stored on ice after they have been caught. When the flesh is pressed firmly with a finger, it must be elastic. If an imprint is left behind in the fish's flesh, then it is no longer fresh.

Crustaceans must also be fresh. In European shops, shrimps, crayfish and similar types of seafood are generally ready-cooked. They are usually boiled by fishermen on their boats as soon as they are caught.
Freshly-caught crustaceans can be identified by:
– firm shells
– a pleasant smell. As with fish, a strong, fishy smell from crustaceans, is likely to indicate that they are not fresh.
Look out for the following signs of freshness with mussels:
– fresh mussels are alive even though their shells remained firmly closed. Any mussel shells which stay open must be discarded straight away. They should close when tapped lightly.
If a mussel stays closed after cooking, it should also be discarded. As with other shellfish, most mussels may be eaten raw, so it is essential to insist on freshness. Fish in a Japanese kitchen is always a pleasure. The following fish are amongst the most popular.

Fish

Bonito. This small blue fish, a member of the tuna family, is low in fat. *Katsuobushi* (bonito flakes), a basic ingredient of fish stock, is made from this fish.

Conger eel has a strong, spicy flavour. The firm flesh is ideal for use in stews.

Flounder and **Halibut** are flatfish with particularly tender flesh and are perfect for grilling.

Mackerel and **Horse Mackerel** are still small in the early spring and that is when they are at their best, served fresh of course. They are fatty fish, which can quickly lose their flavour.

Plaice is another flatfish, a little bigger than the flounder. It is best eaten baked or grilled.

Redfish is good if served with a coating of breadcrumbs.

Salmon. Its delicious meat is ideal in a marinade or grilled. Take care when baking or grilling as the flesh can easily dry out. It needs to be kept moist.

Sardines. Small, fatty fish which are very tasty when grilled or marinated.

Sea Bream or **Red Sea Bream** taste delicious and the **Gilt-head Bream** also tastes superb marinated or grilled.

Tuna comes in two varieties, either red or white. Red tuna is up to three metres long, the white no more than a metre. It tastes best eaten raw in sashimi. The fatty flank slices (toro) are prized ingredients in sushi.

Crustaceans

Crawfish or **Langoustines.** Rather like lobsters in appearance, but no more than 26 cm/10 in long. The best meat is in the tail.

Crabs should be as big as two outstretched hands and contain firm flesh. In our recipes, we use only dressed crabmeat.

Prawns There are the small, transparent kind and the giant ones known as **Scampi** or **Dublin Bay Prawns**

Shrimps are closely related to prawns but they are pink. The smaller and tastier ones are between 5 cm/2 in and 15 cm/6 in long. The flesh should be firm.

Shellfish

Abalone or **Ormers** are a great delicacy and can be eaten raw. They are large ear-shaped shells with beautiful mother-of-pearl interiors.

Cockles have relatives which are not edible, so beachcombers take care.

Scallops are found in various forms. The white flesh and the reddish roe are the best parts to eat.

Sea Urchin eggs or **Sea Urchin roe.** They have a spicy flavour and are ideal for sushi or in marinades. They must be really fresh.

Squid have only a thin cartilage instead of bones, so have a high flesh content in relation to weight.

Tokobushi are a variety of Japanese mussels, which are similar to abalone, if perhaps a little smaller. Prepare as for abalone.

DOBINMUSHI

The correct way to prepare this very special kind of fish soup starter is in an earthenware teapot. The delicious aroma is retained in the pot.

Ingredients
4 medium-sized shrimps
2 okra
50 g/2 oz oyster
mushrooms
1 lime
800 ml/1½ pints
fish stock
salt
1 teaspoon soy sauce
8 peeled gingko nuts
(canned)

Method
Peel and devein the shrimps.
Place them in boiling water and cook for two minutes. Drain well.
Wash the okra and slice it into rings about 5 mm/¼ inch thick. Cut the oyster mushrooms into bite-sized chunks.
Quarter the lime.
Prepare a stand on the table ready for the earthenware teapot and the rice-wine bowl.

Bring the fish stock to the boil adding a little salt. Add soy sauce to taste and then continue to simmer.
Put the okra, the oyster mushrooms and the gingko nuts into the teapots. Add the stock to the teapot. Leave to stand for a few minutes, for the flavours to mingle.
Finally, add the shrimps and it is ready to serve.

To serve:
Slowly pour the soup into the rice wine bowls and squeeze a little lime juice over it.
The shrimps, oyster mushrooms, gingko and okra can be eaten straight from the teapot, alternating with the soup.
Top up the rice wine bowls with the soup as required.

FRIED SHRIMPS IN SOY SAUCE

Method
Wash and devein the shrimps, by gently breaking the shell and removing the flesh with the aid of a toothpick. Leave the shrimps to soak in two tablespoons of sake for about ten minutes.
Dry thoroughly with a cloth and then fry in hot oil (170°C).

Put the six tablespoons of sake, sugar and soy sauce in a saucepan with the fish stock and bring to the boil.
Add the shrimps and cook until the sauce caramelises.

To serve
Arrange the shrimps on a dish.

Ingredients
300 g/11 oz shrimps
8 tablespoons sake
oil for frying
6 tablespoons fish stock
2 tablespoons sugar
4 tablespoons soy sauce

ABALONE WITH GREEN ASPARAGUS

Method
Remove the abalone from their shells, wash thoroughly and then make diamond-shaped cuts in the surface.
Blanch the asparagus in salted water but do not allow it to become soft. Then plunge the asparagus into cold water so that it retains its green colour.
Combine the fish stock with the soy sauce and sugar.

Plunge the abalone into simmering water and then rinse under the cold tap. This helps to remove the surface fats.
Then on a low heat slowly cook the abalone in the fish stock. Finally, remove the abalone from the stock and cut them into slices 5 mm/ ¼ inch thick.

To serve
Mix the abalone and asparagus together and arrange in small mounds on the dish. Pick up the sansho leaves in one hand and then hit it with the other. This is the best way to crush the leaves and to allow them to release their aroma. Sprinkle them over the abalone.

Ingredients
8 abalone
8 asparagus spears
375 ml/13 fl oz fish stock
1 tablespoon soy sauce
2 teaspoons sugar
a handful of sansho leaves

HALIBUT SASHIMI

This dish requires momiji-oroshi, *a Japanese condiment made from grated green horseradish and red peppers. Momiji-oroshi means 'maple'. It is green in the summer and red in the autumn. To prepare sashimi requires great skill, which many Japanese cooks have difficulty mastering, but it is definitely worth a try.*

Ingredients
1 kg/2½ lb halibut
2 bunches of chives
10 umeboshi
200 g/7 oz fish livers
(best ordered in advance
from fishmonger)
salt
100 ml/4 fl oz soy sauce
1 tablespoon lemon juice
125 ml/4 fl oz fish stock
1 shiso leaf
momiji-oroshi

Method
Wash and fillet the halibut and cut into thin strips about 8 cm/3 in long and 5 cm/2 in wide.
Wash the chives and cut them into finger-length pieces.
Remove the stones from the umeboshi and crush the flesh with a spoon.
Quickly poach the fish livers in hot, salted water.
Arrange five or six lengths of chive and a little umeboshi on each of the fish strips, then roll each of them up.
Combine the soy sauce with the lemon juice and fish stock and pour a little into four small bowls.

Lay the fish rolls out on a dish with the shiso leaf in the centre.
Cut the fish livers into attractive shapes and lay them next to the rolls.
Sprinkle with momiji-oroshi (page 155).

To serve
Sashimi is always a self-service course, with everyone dipping their own fish rolls in the sauce.
The sauce can be flavoured with momiji-oroshi if desired.

Halibut sashimi

FISH DUMPLINGS IN VEGETABLE STOCK

Ingredients
200 g/7 oz redfish
200 g/7 oz scampi,
shelled
200 g/7 oz scallops,
white flesh only
2 tablespoons cornflour
3 tablespoons sake
2 teaspoons sesame oil
salt
12 leaves iceberg lettuce
200 g/7 oz broccoli
200 g/7 oz cauliflower
8 fresh shiitake
mushrooms
8 radishes
1 bunch of chives
1 lemon
2½ l/4 pints fish stock
6 tablespoons sake
6 tablespoons soy sauce

Method
Finely chop the redfish, scampi and scallops with a sharp knife.
Add the cornflour, sake, sesame oil and salt to the chopped fish and mix thoroughly.
Wash the iceberg lettuce leaves and blanch them in salted water for a few seconds.
Make a dozen small round dumplings from the chopped fish and then wrap each one in a lettuce leaf.
Break the cauliflower and broccoli into florets.
Clean the mushrooms and radishes. Remove the stalks from the mushrooms.
Cut the chives into small pieces with scissors and slice the lemon into eight segments. Arrange them separately in small bowls.

In a large clay pot, mix the fish stock with the sake, salt and soy sauce. Fill the pot to two-thirds full with the stock, bring it to the boil and then leave it to stand on a hotplate.
Gradually add the vegetables to the stock in sequence according to their cooking times. Finally, add the fish dumplings to the stew a few at a time. They only need to cook for a few minutes.

To serve
Ladle the dumplings, vegetables and stock from the pot. The diners can flavour their portions according to taste with the chives and lemon.
If the liquid reduces too much, it can be thinned with a little more stock.
A little cooked rice or a few noodles can be added to the vegetables and fish dumplings, to make a more filling soup. A sprinkle of soy sauce will add extra flavour.

ABALONE WITH BROAD BEANS

In Japan, abalone are often just blanched in hot water and eaten raw, or at least only partly-cooked. In this recipe, the cooking time has been increased slightly.

Method

Sprinkle half a teaspoon of salt on the abalone, rub in with a dry cloth and then wash thoroughly. Salt the abalone again, pour the sake over it and leave to stand in a small saucepan over a low heat for about 15 minutes. Discard the shells and pat the meat dry with paper towels. Cut the abalone into little finger-sized pieces.

Blanch the broad bean pods in hot water for a few seconds. Remove the outer skin from the beans and cut each one into four.
Mix the wasabi thoroughly with one and a half teaspoons of water.

To serve

Divide the abalone and beans into four small bowls and add a little soy sauce to each portion. Put some of the wasabi on the edge of the dish. Coat the slices of abalone with wasabi and then dip them in the soy sauce.

Ingredients
6 abalone
salt
2 tablespoons sake
4 extra large, fresh broad bean pods
1 teaspoon powdered wasabi
2 teaspoons soy sauce

WHITE JAPONICA

Method

Cut the conger eel in half lengthways. Make slits through the flesh at 5 mm/¼ inch intervals. Cut each piece in half again to make four pieces.
Pour some water into a saucepan, add the kombu and heat. Just before the water boils, remove the kombu and add the conger eel pieces with a little salt.
As soon as the eel is cooked and the cuts opens up like a flower, remove the fish and drain it well.
Wash the spinach thoroughly and blanch it in salted water.
Drain the spinach and cut it into finger-sized shreds.

Bring the fish stock to the boil with some salt and soy sauce.

To serve

Arrange the spinach and the conger eel in four wooden bowls so that they look like leaves around a flower. Pour the stock over them and then add a little umeboshi to the fish. They should resemble white japonica. Finally, sprinkle the contents of the bowls with a little chopped dillweed.

Ingredients
350 g/12 oz conger eel
5 × 5 cm/2 in pieces kombu
100 g/4 oz spinach
600 ml/1 pint fish stock
1 teaspoon soy sauce
1 teaspoon umeboshi
1 bunch of dillweed, chopped

REDFISH WITH ASPARAGUS

Ingredients

400 g/14 oz redfish fillet
12 asparagus spears
10 × 10 cm/4 in kombu
30 g/1 oz katsuobushi
1 teaspoon salt
1 teaspoon soy sauce
2 tablespoons cornmeal
Rice wine vinegar
6 sansho leaves

Method

Slice the fish fillet. Trim any woody bits from base of the asparagus stems.

Wipe the kombu with a damp cloth to ensure no grains of sand remain. Leave the seaweed to soak in 500 ml/16 fl oz of water for 30 minutes, then bring the water to the boil. When it has started to simmer, remove the kombu.

Put the katsuobushi in the broth and bring it to the boil. Remove the saucepan from the heat and leave the stock to stand for a few minutes. Strain the stock through a sieve and then add salt and soy sauce to taste.

Add a few drops of vinegar to some water in a pan, bring to the boil and cook the asparagus. Sprinkle some salt on the fish fillet, dip it in the cornmeal and then quickly immerse in boiling salted water. The fish can then be left to drain in a colander. Finish cooking the fish pieces in a steamer.

Remove the asparagus from the vinegar water then poach it in the katsuobushi-flavoured stock.

Pick up the sansho leaves with one hand and tap it with the other. This crushes the leaf and releases the sansho's delicate aroma.

To serve

Arrange the redfish and the asparagus in a bowl. Pour some of the stock over them and finally garnish with the sansho leaves.

MARINATED BONITO

Ingredients

400 g/14 oz bonito fillets
½ clove garlic
3 tablespoons soy sauce
1 teaspoon powdered wasabi
8 leaves of shiso or mint

Method

Dice the bonito fillets into 2 cm/¼ inch cubes and cut the garlic clove into wafer-thin slices. Leave to marinate in the soy sauce for about ten minutes.

Mix the wasabi thoroughly with one teaspoon of water.

To serve

Remove the fish from the marinade and wrap it in shiso leaves. Divide the parcels between the four bowls and complete the dish by adding a little wasabi to the middle of each bowl.

CRAB STEW

Kanimiso is an aromatic, grey-green substance found in the corners of crab shells. It is regarded as a delicacy. Kanimiso gives this dish extra relish.

Method
Cut the crabmeat into bite-sized portions.
Peel the radish, wash the leeks and the spinach. Slice the radish thinly and slice the leeks into julienne strips. Each piece of leek should be about 3 cm/1 in long.
Fry the leek and the radish in hot oil for a few moments.
Cut the ends of the stems from the enoki mushrooms. Carefully separate the mushrooms and then carefully wash them.

Take the kanimiso out of the crab shells and dilute it with the sake. Stir a little of the red and white miso together with some stock and add to the blended kanimiso-and-sake mixture. Then pour the sauce into a saucepan, add the remaining miso and the fish stock. Bring to the boil for a minute or two. The miso will give off a subtle aroma; take care that the liquid does not boil away and dry up. Ensure that none of the ingredients in this recipe are over-cooked.

To serve
Add half the crabmeat and half the vegetables to the stock and bring to the boil. When the vegetables are tender, put the pan on a hotplate. Remove the ingredients from the stock with chopsticks and place them in small bowls. When they have been eaten, repeat the process with the remaining crab and vegetables and re-fill the bowls.

Ingredients
400 g/14 oz dressed crabmeat
1 white radish
250 g/9 oz spinach
2 leeks
2 tablespoons oil
1 packet enoki mushrooms
4 crab shells
1 teaspoon sake
2 l/3½ pints fish stock
3 tablespoons white miso
2 tablespoons red miso

PRAWN STEW WITH SCALLOPS

Ginger and peppers give this seafood stew a special piquancy.
Japanese dried red peppers are only the size of a fingernail.

Ingredients
4 prawns
200 g/7 oz watercress
150 g/6 oz mushrooms
30 g/1 oz fresh ginger
8 scallops
a bunch of chives
1 small dry red chili
pepper
salt
2 l/3½ pints chicken
stock
8 tablespoons soy sauce
2 tablespoons lemon
juice

Method
Remove the prawns from their shells and discard the vein. Cut the flesh into 3-cm/1-inch sections. Rinse the watercress in cold water, then wipe it dry and divide it into smaller bunches. Clean the mushrooms thoroughly and then halve each one. Peel the ginger and slice it very thinly. Clean the scallops carefully.
Chop the chives. Seed the pepper and slice it into rings.
Mix the soy sauce with the lemon juice and divide it between the four bowls.

Put the chicken stock into a flameproof casserole with the salt and ginger. As soon as the stock boils, add the prepared vegetables and the prawns. Allow the stew to cook slowly. Finally, sprinkle it with the chives and the red pepper.

To serve
Put the pot on a hotplate to keep it warm and serve the stew. Remove the ingredients from the stock and dip them in the blended soy sauce and lemon juice. Take care not to overcook these delicate ingredients. Never allow the liquid to boil too vigorously.

Prawn stew
with scallops

MACKEREL FRIED IN OIL

Ingredients
*400 g/14 oz mackerel
fillet
1 dried red chili pepper
3¼ tablespoons soy
sauce
1 tablespoon sake
2 teaspoons cornflour
oil for frying
1 lemon*

Method
Wipe the mackerel and pat it dry, then slice it into strips 2 cm/1 in by 3 cm/1½ in. Seed and chop the red pepper.
Combine 3 tablespoons sake with the chopped red pepper and the cornflour and marinate the mackerel for 20 minutes. Turn the fillets frequently to ensure that they are all well-coated.

Heat the oil in a frying-pan and fry the mackerel until it is golden-brown. Before serving, drain the fillets thoroughly on absorbent paper.

To serve
Serve the fried mackerel on four plates and garnish with lemon slices.

GRILLED TUNA

Ingredients
*2 tablespoons soy sauce
1½ tablespoons mirin
4 × 100 g/4 oz tuna
steaks
100 ml/4 fl oz sake
2 tablespoons sugar
1 dried red chili pepper
8 radishes
salt*

Method
Mix two tablespoons of soy sauce with one tablespoon of mirin and marinate the tuna steaks in the mixture for 30 minutes. Turn the steaks over from time to time. Seed the dried red chili pepper and chop it finely. Combine the sake, the rest of the mirin, 2 tablespoons sugar and finely chopped red pepper and bring to the boil. As soon as the liquid boils, remove the pan from the heat and leave the contents to cool. Clean the radishes and cut them in half in a zigzag pattern, so that they look like roses. Lightly salt them, leave for five minutes, dry them with kitchen paper and then add to the marinade. Marinate for 15 minutes.

Remove the fish from the marinade and leave it to drain for a few minutes. Preheat the grill. Arrange the fish in an ovenproof dish and grill for 7 or 8 minutes on each side, or until cooked through.

To serve
Drain the marinated radishes and arrange them on the four plates with the fish.

SALMON CASSEROLE

*The delicate flavour and firm texture of salmon make a superb meal,
so why all these extra ingredients? Well, there is a good reason for
them, they really add something special to the 'king of fish'. This
delicious casserole has to be experienced to be believed.*

Method

Salt the salmon and cut it into 2 cm/1 in cubes. Wash the endives and
slice them in half lengthways.

Chop the leeks diagonally into 5 cm/2 in lengths. Slice the carrots into
5 mm/¼ inch slices and the radish into 8 mm/½ inch slices.

Cut the tofu into 2.5 cm/1 in cubes and chop up the konyaku.

Trim the roots from the turnip leaves, wash the leaves and tear them
into small pieces.

Wipe the kombu with a damp cloth to remove any grains of sand, then
use scissors to cut it into four strips. Put the kombu in water and warm
over medium heat, but remove the strips before the water boils. Mix
some red miso with a little stock and then return to the pan with the
sugar and the mirin.

Add all the other ingredients to the stock except the turnip leaves, and
cook only until the texture is firm and crunchy. Last of all, add the turnip
leaves.

To serve

Serve the stew in small bowls, topping up as required. Sansho and
shichimi togarashi may be added for extra flavour.

Ingredients

*500 g/1 lb 2 oz fresh
salmon*
coarse salt
5 endives
4 leeks
*100 g/4 oz young
carrots*
*250 g/9 oz white
radishes*
200 g/7 oz tofu
a piece of konyaku
*a bunch of spring turnip
leaves*
10 × 10 cm/4 in kombu
150 g/6 oz red miso
1 tablespoon sugar
2½ tablespoons mirin
*1 tablespoon sansho
(optional)*
*1 tablespoon shichimi
togarashi (optional)*

*Overleaf:
Salmon stew*

GRILLED SQUID WITH SEA URCHIN ROE

Ingredients
250 g/9 oz squid
salt
1 tablespoon sake
2 tablespoons sea urchin roe
1 egg yolk
4 stalks of watercress
1 teaspoon black poppyseeds

Method
Wash the squid thoroughly, discard the ink sac and cartilage and slice the squid in half lengthways. Make some incisions on the upper side. Rub a little salt and a few drops of sake into it.
Mix the sea urchin roe with the egg yolk.
Thread the squid on to skewers.
Wash the watercress and drain it well.

Lay the skewers of squid on a sheet of aluminium foil and grill the cut side of the squid. Turn them over and lightly brown the other side. Twist the skewers from time to time, so that their contents can be removed easily. Brush the sauce over the cut side of the squid and place under the grill. When the sauce dries, repeat the process. Do this two or three times, but take care that the surface does not burn. Remove the skewer and then cut the squid into pieces 3 cm/1 in wide by 5 cm/2 in long.

To serve
Arrange the squid on four plates and garnish with watercress. Sprinkle poppy seeds over the squid.

SQUID WITH CAVIAR

This dish has only three ingredients. It is most important to slice the squid as thinly as possible. To do this, use a very sharp knife and freeze the fish.

Ingredients
200 g/7 oz prepared fresh squid
1 lemon, rind peeled
2 tablespoons caviar
2 teaspoons soy sauce

Method
Halve the squid lengthways, then cut each half again into two or three pieces. Each piece should be no thicker than 4 mm/¼ inch.
Slice the cut sections into paper-thin slices.
Cut the lemon peel into small rectangles about 3 mm/¼ inch wide and 6 mm/½ inch long. Then score them down the middle, fold them back along the score, so that they look like pine needles.

To serve
Combine the squid, caviar and lemon peel and arrange in four small bowls.
If required, flavour with a little soy sauce.

FISH STEW WITH RICE WINE

There are three types of sea-bream. For this dish, the gilt-head bream is used. It has a particularly distinctive flavour.

Method

Remove the head and scales from the bream and discard them.

Fillet the fish carefully, reserving the bones.

Cut the head and flesh into slices 2 cm/1 in thick. Sprinkle with salt and leave to stand for 15 minutes. Heat sufficient water to cover the fish and poach in hot, but not boiling, water (85°C/185°F) for a few minutes. Leave to drain.

Separate the Chinese cabbage carefully and slice the leaves into finger-wide strips.

Chop the turnip leaves into short lengths; blanch both vegetables for 3 minutes and drain thoroughly. Roll up the cabbage leaves.

Thinly slice the turnip. Clean the shiitake mushrooms and discard the stalks. Dice the tofu.

Cut the spring onions into thin rings and soak them in cold water. Grate the radish.

Slice the lime thinly.

Fill a saucepan two thirds full with the diluted sake and add a pinch of salt. Add the fish bones and the kombu. Boil up the liquid, take out the bones and the kombu and strain the remainder through a sieve to remove any solids.

Add the fish slices, the rolled Chinese cabbage leaves, the turnip leaves, the slices of white turnip, the tofu and the shiitake mushrooms.

To serve

Serve portions in small bowls and flavour them with soy sauce, spring onions, white radish and lime juice.

Ingredients

1 small sea-bream
(about 300 g/11 oz)
salt
1 Chinese cabbage
(Chinese leaves or bok choy)
a bunch of spring turnip leaves
1 turnip
200 g/7 oz tofu
8 fresh shiitake mushrooms
750 ml diluted sake
(half sake, half water)
5 × 5 cm/2 in kombu
2 spring onions
100 g/4 oz white radish
(daikon or mooli)
1 lime
8 tablespoons soy sauce
Lime juice for sprinkling

MOCK SEA URCHINS

Making these sweet 'sea urchins' requires quite a lot of hard work, but the result is spectacular. Not only do they look good, they taste delicious.

Ingredients

12 sweet chestnuts
1 tablespoon sugar
6 × 6 cm/2½ in kombu
30 g/1 oz flour
700g/1½ lb shrimps
salt
1 tablespoon mirin
1 egg white
12 radishes
100 g/4 oz somen noodles
About 500 ml/16 fl oz oil for frying

Method

Make deep slits on the flat sides of the sweet chestnuts. Place the chestnuts in a saucepan with just enough water to cover them and bring them to the boil.

Boil for 3 minutes, then remove them from the water and peel them, discarding the shells and the inner skin. Return them to the boiling water and simmer for 20 minutes. Put two tablespoons of cold water and a tablespoon of sugar in a heavy-based pan and add the chestnuts. Simmer them very gently until soft.

Soak the kombu for 20 minutes in a 250 ml/8 fl oz water. Transfer the kombu and water to the heat and simmer for 10 minutes. Use a mortar and pestle to crush the kombu into the flour until it forms a paste. Reserve the paste.

Purée the shrimps then combine them with the salt, mirin, egg white and 4 tablespoons of the kombu paste. Beat gently to make a creamy mixture.

Cut the radishes into marble-sized balls about 1 cm/½ in. in diameter. Shape the shrimp mixture over them, so that you have 12 little 'dumplings' with the radishes at the centre.

Spread out the somen noodles on a work surface and lightly roll the 'dumplings' in them until a 'spiny sea-urchin' emerges.

Heat the oil in deep-fryer until it is hot enough to fry a 2.5 cm/1 in cube of bread in 60 seconds. Deep-fry the 'urchins' on high heat for 2 to 3 minutes until golden-brown. Remove them carefully and drain them.

To serve

Turn the 'urchin' on its back and carefully open up the prawn coating with a small, sharp knife. Remove the radish and replace it with a sweet chestnut. The 'urchins' are best eaten when they have cooled to room temperature.

Mock sea urchin

MACKEREL IN MISO SAUCE

Ingredients

*400 g/14 oz mackerel
fillet
salt
15 g/½ oz ginger root
4 spring onions
80 ml/3 fl oz sake
100 ml/4 fl oz fish stock
3 tablespoons sugar
1 teaspoon soy sauce
1 teaspoon red miso*

Method

Cut the mackerel fillets into slices 3 cm/1 in wide and make cuts in the skin.

Lightly salt the fish and leave it for ten minutes, then put the pieces in a colander and scald them with boiling water.

Peel the ginger root, reserving the skin, and grate finely. Place the grated ginger in a serving bowl.

Wash the spring onions and cut them into 3 cm/1 in lengths.

Bring the sake to the boil, then add the fish stock and the soy sauce. Bring to the boil again add the ginger skin and the mackerel, skin-side down.

When the stock comes to the boil again, cover the fish with aluminium foil and poach on a low heat for a further five minutes, so that it absorbs the stock.

Dilute the miso with a little sauce. Pour it over the fish and continue to cook gently for about two minutes. Shake the pan occasionally to prevent the miso from burning. Finally add the spring onions and bring the stock back to the boil.

To serve

Remove the fish from the stock and serve on four plates. Pour the sauce containing the spring onions over it. Sprinkle with the grated ginger.

BRAISED PLAICE

Method

Remove the fish head and fillet it carefully. Remove and discard the skin and cut the fish into paper-thin slices.
Prepare the dandelion leaves by washing them thoroughly and tearing them into 5-cm/2- inch pieces.
Wash the chives and chop finely.
Combine the soy sauce with the lemon juice to make ponzu sauce.

Bring the kombu stock to the boil in a flameproof casserole. When the stock comes to the boil, remove it from the heat and pour it into a hot serving bowl to keep warm.
Arrange the fish on a platter with the dandelion leaves.

To serve

Serve the ponzu sauce, the chives and the momiji-oroshi (page 155) in side-dishes. Add the vegetables to the stock and return to the boil. To eat, use chopsticks to dip the fish slices in the stock for a few seconds and then again in the ponzu sauce and the other side dishes.

Ingredients

1 plaice or flounder
(600 g - 800 g/1½-1¾ lb)
100 g/4 oz dandelion
leaves
1 small bunch of chives
350 ml/12 fl oz soy
sauce
3 tablespoons lemon
juice
500 ml/16 fl oz kombu
stock
momiji-oroshi

HORSE MACKEREL IN WASABI SAUCE

Other types of mackerel can be used instead of horse mackerel.

Method

Wash the mackerel and fillet it carefully. Make doubly sure that all bones have been removed. Heat the nori gently in a frying pan, then crumble it in a cloth.
Chop the chives finely.
Mix the wasabi with the soy sauce. Place the fish on the grill pan and grill for 3 minutes on each side. Break the mackerel into smaller pieces by hand.

To serve

Combine the fish with the crumbled nori and wasabi sauce.
Serve in four small bowls and sprinkle with the chives.

Ingredients

250 g/9 oz horse
mackerel
½ nori sheet
1 small bunch of chives
1 tablespoon wasabi
(Japanese horseradish)
2 tablespoons soy sauce

SPICY SARDINES

Sardines prepared in this way can justifiably be called 'spicy'.
The special blend of spices helps the fish to remain juicy and tender.
The longer they are marinated, the more distinctive the flavour.

Ingredients

12 fresh sardines (each about 50 g/2 oz)
50 g/2 oz white radish (daikon or mooli)
3 umeboshi
1 pinch katsuobushi
4 shiso leaves
2 tablespoons oil
1½ tablespoons sesame seed
1½ tablespoons soy sauce
1½ tablespoons sake
1 tablespoon red miso
1 tablespoon sugar
2 tablespoons finely chopped spring onion
½ teaspoon Cayenne pepper

Method

Heat the oven to 170°C/350°F/Gas mark 3.
Remove the heads from the sardines, fillet them and rinse carefully. Cut the radish into strips 1 cm/½ in wide and 5 cm/2 in long.
Stone the umeboshi and chop finely. Mix it with the radish and then sprinkle on the katsuobushi. Wash the shiso leaves carefully and then leave to dry on a kitchen towel.
Heat 1 tablespoon of oil in a frying-pan and toast the sesame seeds. Combine them with the soy sauce, sake, miso and sugar. Finally add the spring onions and Cayenne pepper.

Leave the sardines to marinate in this mixture for about 30 minutes. Crinkle some aluminium foil and brush it with the rest of the oil, so that the sardine skin does not stick to it. Place the sardines on the foil and pour a little of the sauce over them. Wrap the foil tightly around the sardines and bake in the oven for five minutes.

To serve

Remove the foil from the sardines and arrange three sardines on each plate. Arrange the radish strips with umeboshi on a shiso leaf and serve as a side-dish. It may be a good idea to dip the sardines once more in the marinade before eating. The radish salad and the marinade also go very well with squid.

COCKLES WITH SWISS CHARD

When purchasing shellfish, it is important to check that the shells are closed. If cockles in the shell are not available, clams or mussels can be used instead.

Method

Steep the cockles in salt water for at least 1 hour, so that they eject any sand. Place them in a colander and rinse under the cold tap.

Put the cockles in a saucepan, add 60 ml/2 fl oz sake, cover and steam over a high heat until all the shells have opened. As with all varieties of shellfish, discard any which do not open.

Remove the cockles and strain the liquid into a bowl through a sieve lined with muslin or cheesecloth.

Wash the Swiss chard and blanch it in hot salted water for a few moments. Plunge immediately into cold water and drain.

Cut the chard leaves into 5-cm/2-inch lengths.

Put the fish stock in a pan with 125 ml/4 fl oz of the shellfish cooking liquid, the sugar, the mirin, the soy sauce and salt and bring it all to the boil.

Add the chard, bring back to the boil and return the cockles to the pot to reheat them.

To serve

Serve the cockles with the stock and chard in four small bowls.

Ingredients

500 g/1 lb 2 oz fresh cockles in the shell
3 tablespoons sake
2 bunches Swiss chard
250 ml/8 fl oz stock
2 teaspoons sugar
½ tablespoon mirin
2 tablespoons soy sauce
salt

VEGETABLES

THE HEALTHY WAY TO PREPARE VEGETABLES

Fresh vegetables are an essential part of a healthy diet. They provide vital vitamins, minerals and fibre but contain only a few calories. The fresher the vegetables, the higher the vitamin and mineral content. The longer vegetables are exposed to air, light and heat, the faster the goodness disappears. That is why it is so important to eat vegetables when they are fresh. Vegetables play an important part in Japanese cuisine. They are often eaten raw, cut into wafer-thin slices or made into the most beautiful arrangements. They feature in a variety of table decorations. For instance, crane may be carved out of a white radish or a flower arrangement made from a selection of vegetables. The usual way to cook vegetables is to steam them. This cooks the vegetables right through, with the added advantage that no fat is required. The Japanese way is to first lay some seaweed in a bamboo basket, and then to place this over a saucepan containing boiling water. More baskets may be stacked on top. The steam is prevented from escaping by placing a cloth and then the lid over the top basket. Steamed vegetables are deliciously tender. The Japanese like to flavour them with soy sauce or sake. A cup and a plate placed inside a tall saucepan are a simple alternative to the steamer. Put the cup upside down in a saucepan, fill the saucepan with water to a depth of 4 centimetres/2 inches, put a plate on the cup and bring the water to the boil. This rather precarious arrangement is best suited to cooking small portions. Tempura is a dish which brings the best out of vegetables. Morsels of vegetable are dipped in the batter and then fried in hot oil. Whichever method of cooking is used, the Japanese treat their vegetables with care. A short cooking time is the secret of success. One completely different approach, of course, is to preserve them with salt and herbs. Chopped vegetables are mixed with salt and a variety of herbs and then pressed under a heavy weight for 24 hours. The liquid is drained off and the vegetables are served as seasonings.

VEGETABLES, MUSHROOMS AND NUTS

Asparagus must be one of the tastiest vegetables. All varieties whether white, green or purple, should have firm stems, but the tips will need careful handling. Any woody parts of the spear must be removed before cooking. Green asparagus is the best type for Japanese dishes.

Aubergines have shiny purple skins and creamy flesh. They must not be eaten raw. They can be grilled or fried, but must first be sliced, salted and left for a while to drain, to remove some of the bitterness. Japanese aubergines are longer and slenderer than the type usually sold in Europe.

Bamboo shoots. There are over 200 varieties of bamboo shoots. They are, in fact, tiny seedlings and are dug out of the ground in early spring. Bamboo shoots are the basic spring-time vegetable in Japan, though it is hard to find fresh shoots on sale in Europe. However, they can usually be bought in tins.

Broad beans are eaten during the early summer months for their distinctive flavour. They should be boiled for a few minutes before serving.

Carrots are a tasty root vegetable which can either be served raw in salads or boiled as a vegetable. They can also be cut into various shapes and used as a garnish. Their colour is very much appreciated by the Japanese.

Chinese leaves (Chinese leaves or **Bok choy)** is often used in fondues and stews. The Japanese preserve it for the winter.

Chives belong to the onion family and are similar to leeks in taste and in the way they can be used.

Chrysanthemum leaves are regarded by the Japanese as a vegetable. These leaves are shredded, quickly blanched and eaten in a salad.

Cucumbers should always be firm and of an even green colour. They are not a strong-tasting vegetable and so are very versatile in Japanese cuisine.

Dandelion leaves have been re-discovered in Europe. They have a bitter taste similar to chicory. They lose some of their bitterness, but none of their flavour, if they are steamed like spinach.

Edamame are young soya beans. They are often served as an hors d'œuvre. They should be blanched for a few moments before serving,

Garlic can be eaten raw or cooked. It gives just the right aroma to so many dishes.

Horseradish. European horseradish has long, thick roots. It is a brownish-yellow colour on the outside, but white on the inside. It has a sharp, hot taste and a strong smell and is usually sold ready grated, as a paste or in jars.

Iceberg lettuce is popular in Japan. The firm leaves can also be steamed.

Kabu is Japanese kohlrabi and is similar to many European varieties. It has a floury texture when cooked.

Lotus root. The hollow roots of the water-lily can be marinated raw, boiled, steamed or deep-fried. If they are cut into thin slices, they can be stuffed.

Mangetout are the only variety of peas eaten with their pods. These young, fresh pods have a superbly delicate flavour.

Marrows and **Pumpkins** come in over 800 different varieties. The Japanese pumpkin has a sweet, nutty flavour.

Okra look like little green peppers and can be between 4 cm/2 in and 15 cm/6 in long. They taste mild, slightly bitter, with a little sour spiciness. The taste has been likened to that of beans or gooseberries.

Potatoes are a versatile vegetable. In Japanese cuisine they are accompanied by soy sauce and mirin.

Chili peppers have small, pointed pods. A tiny quantity can give a dish a real bite.

Salsify (Scorzonera) is often described as the poor man's asparagus. It is a black-skinned root with white flesh. Peeled and boiled the roots have a delicate, distinctly nutty flavour. Japanese salsify resembles the European variety only in appearance; it tastes stronger and spicier than its European cousins.

Spinach should be eaten fresh. The young leaves are delicious and are ideal in salads, fondues and stews.

Spring onions are one of the many varieties of onion. The white bulb and part of the tender green stem may be eaten. The Japanese chop them finely and use them as a flavouring.

Spring turnips are a root vegetable in Europe, but the Japanese prefer the turnip tops. The young leaves are either pickled or blanched and served in salads.

Sweet corn is like bamboo and is a grain crop. It can be processed into meal, oil or flour. Whole corn cobs can be boiled, grilled or steamed.

Sweet Potatoes are large tubers with reddish skins. Like all potatoes, they can be eaten with or without their skins, boiled or fried. As the name suggests, they have a sweet taste and are often eaten as desserts.

Swiss Chard is related to beetroot but, like spinach, it is the leaves which are eaten. It has a spicier and more distinctive flavour than spinach. The stems and stalks are prepared like scorzonera.

Watercress grows in running water. The round leaves and stalks have a distinctive peppery taste.

White Radish (known in Japanese as **Daikon** and in the Caribbean as **Mooli**) is a large root vegetable. The skin is creamy and the flesh is brilliant white; the flavour is mildly peppery. White radish can be eaten raw and marinated. Tsuma, white radish cut into julienne strips, is an important accompaniment for sashimi. Grated white radish is used for flavouring tempura.

Zenmai are the young shoots of the zenmai grass or the royal fern which grows on river banks and on grassland. The shoots are pulled and then they are flexed manually to weakened the fibres. The slightly bitter flavour of zenmai is appreciated by the Japanese. This grass is available in Europe only in dried form.

Mushrooms

Cultivated Mushrooms of the European type come in several varieties. There are the small, white mushrooms and the large brown ones. The large, brown

Field Mushroom is much tastier than the white cultivated mushroom.

Enoki mushrooms have small caps on long stems, sometimes as long as 10 cm/4 ins. They grow in clusters and are similar in taste to the European cultivated mushroom.

Matsutake mushrooms are the best Japanese mushrooms and are similar to the European Oyster Mushroom.

Shiitake mushrooms have large, fleshy caps varying in colour from grey to brown, to reddish-brown. They need not be washed since they are cultivated, but should be wiped clean with a cloth or soft brush, and the stems trimmed. After cooking they should be well-seasoned. Unlike most other mushrooms, the flavour improves when the mushrooms are dried.

Shimeji mushrooms are small and similar to cultivated mushrooms. They grow in clusters and have longish stems.

Nuts

Chestnuts are often cooked after being shelled, but with the skins left on. They are roasted or boiled, and peeled after cooking. They have a strong, nutty, aromatic flavour.

Gingko Nuts. You will probably have to buy these in tins, as fresh ones are hard to come by. The fresh nuts are a deep green colour and are much firmer than canned nuts, which have been heat-treated. Preserved nuts are yellowish in colour and have a less distinctive flavour.

Peanuts, still in their skins, but without their shells, can be used as a basis for tasty sauces.

VEGETABLE SOUP WITH MISO

Ingredients
4 spring onions
*1 potato (about 75 g/
3 oz)*
75 g/3 oz pumpkin
100 g/4 oz red miso
*500 ml/16 fl oz fish
stock*

Method
Cut the spring onion into thin strips lengthways. Wash and peel the potato, and slice it into strips 5 mm/¼ inch wide and 5 cm/2 in long. Steep in cold water.
Peel the pumpkin and slice the flesh into strips the same size as the potatoes.

Put the pumpkin and potato in a pan with the fish stock and simmer for 20 minutes. Add the onions 8 minutes before they are ready.
Dilute the miso with a little stock and then add to the pan. Reheat but do not allow the stock to re-boil.

To serve
Divide the soup between the four small bowls.

VEGETABLE SOUP

Ingredients
150 g/6 oz salsify
1 teaspoon rice vinegar
100 g/4 oz potatoes
*100 g/4 oz white radish
(daikon or mooli)*
50 g/2 oz carrots
1 leek
250 g/9 oz tofu
*4 fresh shiitake
mushrooms*
2 teaspoons oil
1½ l/2¼ pints fish stock
4 teaspoons soy sauce
shichimi togarashi

Method
Peel the salsify and cut into wedges 2.5 cm/1 in long. Soak the wedges in cold water with the vinegar, so that they do not discolour.
Peel the potatoes, radish and carrots. Cut these vegetables into quarters and then slice them thinly.
Wash the leek thoroughly and cut it diagonally into thin slices. Dice the tofu into 2 cm/1 in cubes, then place in a sieve and press through the mesh. Wipe the shiitake mushrooms and trim the stems. Slice the caps thinly. Heat the oil in a saucepan and fry the salsify, potatoes, radish and carrots for one minute. Add the fish stock and flavour with soy sauce. Reduce the heat and simmer for 5 minutes. Add the tofu and the mushrooms and allow continue to cook for another two minutes. Remove the pan from the heat and add the leek slices.

To serve
Fill four small bowls with the soup and season with shichimi togarashi.

PICKLED SPRING TURNIP TOPS

This is an unusual way to prepare turnip leaves – but the result is delicious.

Ingredients
10 × 10 cm/4 in kombu
2 tablespoons rice vinegar
400 g/14 oz turnip leaves
100 g/4 oz baby carrots
2 teaspoons coarse salt

Method
Wipe the kombu with a damp cloth to remove any sand. Use a pair of kitchen scissors to cut the kombu into julienne strips. Soak for at least 12 hours in rice vinegar.
Rinse the turnip leaves well and cut them into 3 cm/1 in long strips. Wash the carrots and cut them to the same size as the kombu.

Put the turnip leaves, carrots and kombu in a shallow bowl or dish and sprinkle with the salt. Cover the pan, using a wooden board slightly smaller than the diameter of the pan, press down the vegetables with a weight, a heavy tin for example, and leave it to stand for at least twelve hours.

To serve
Remove the pickle from the pan and serve in a bowl.

LOTUS ROOTS WITH PLUM SAUCE

This is an amazingly simple recipe – remarkable not just for the few ingredients it requires, but also for its unique flavour.

Ingredients
200 g/7 oz lotus roots
4 umeboshi
1 tablespoon sugar
1½ tablespoons soy sauce
1 teaspoon mirin

Method
Clean and peel the lotus roots, cut into thin slices and then cook in boiling water.
Remove the stones from the umeboshi and pass them through a sieve. Mix well with the sugar, soy sauce and mirin.

Mix the lotus roots with the sauce and leave for ten minutes.

To serve
Serve in four small bowls.

VEGETABLE STEW WITH WHITE RADISH, PUMPKIN AND PEANUT SAUCE

It takes a long time to prepare the peanuts but the lengthy cooking is necessary to make a delicious sauce. If the peanuts are puréed first, this helps to make the sauce creamier.

Method

Peel the white radish and cut it into pieces 3 cm/1 in thick. Smooth off all the corners. Put the kombu, rice and prepared white radish into a saucepan with water to cover, cover the pan, and bring to the boil. Reduce the heat to low and gently for 1 hour.

Wash the pumpkin thoroughly, peel it and cut it in half. Discard the seeds and cut the flesh into cubes. Make cuts in the flesh, so that the stock can permeate it.

Boil the peanuts in the water until the skins are soft. Drain off the water, remove the skins and simmer the nuts for another 3 hours.

Put the pumpkin in a saucepan with a 250 ml/8 fl oz of the fish stock, bring to the boil and cook on medium heat for 10 minutes. Add 1 tablespoon of the mirin, a pinch of salt and a teaspoon of sake, then cook for another ten minutes.

Clean the mangetout peas and blanch them briefly in boiling water.

Take 500 ml/16 fl oz of the fish stock and bring to the boil, adding the rest of the mirin, the soy sauce and the sugar. Mix the cornflour or arrowroot with a tablespoon of water and then add to the stock. Stir until the sauce thickens, then add the peanuts.

To serve

Serve the white radish, the pumpkin and mangetout in four small bowls, then pour the sauce over them.

Ingredients

300-400g/6-7 oz white radish (daikon or mooli)
10 × 10 cm/4 in kombu
1 tablespoon rice
200-250g/7-9 oz pumpkin
120 g/5 oz raw peanuts (shelled but in their skins)
375 ml/13 fl oz fish stock
2 tablespoons mirin
salt
1 teaspoon sake
60g/2 oz mangetout
2 tablespoons soy sauce
1 tablespoon sugar
1½ tablespoons cornflour or arrowroot

Swiss chard stew

Ginger juice is the liquid from the pickled red ginger root known as Beni shoga. It can be bought in oriental grocers.

Ingredients
200 g/7 oz mackerel fillets
100 ml/4 fl oz soy sauce
100 ml/4 fl oz sake
1 teaspoon ginger juice
300 g/11 oz Swiss chard
1 lime
2 teaspoons cornflour or arrowroot
oil for frying
1.5 l/2¼ pints fish stock
3 tablespoons mirin

Method
Rinse the mackerel fillets, pat them dry and slice them into strips the size of matchsticks.
Combine 1½ tablespoons of soy sauce with 2 teaspoons of the sake and the ginger juice. Marinate the fish in this mixture for 20 minutes, turning occasionally.
Clean the Swiss chard and cut it into strips about 10 cm/4 in long. Wash the lime and cut it into quarters.

Dry the fish with a cloth and sprinkle it with the cornflour or arrowroot. Heat the oil until it just starts to smoke and fry the fish until it is golden-brown. Drain well.
Put the fish stock in a saucepan with the remaining soy sauce, add the mirin and the sake and bring to the boil. Add salt to taste. Finally, add the vegetables and fried fish and bring the soup to a brisk boil. The vegetables should still be crunchy in texture when the soup is ready.

To serve
Serve in bowls with the lime quarters. Sprinkle with lime juice to taste.

Pumpkin with prawn sauce

Ingredients
½ Hokkaido pumpkin or Japanese variety
5 prawns
500 ml/16 fl oz fish stock
1½ teaspoons soy sauce
salt
½ teaspoon mirin
1 tablespoon cornflour

Method
Peel the pumpkin. Cut it first into eight long strips and then again to form bite-sized chunks. Make deep cuts on one side of each piece. Cook the pumpkin in boiling water, making sure the flesh does not become too soft. Shell and devein the prawns. Cut the flesh of the prawns into small pieces and poach for a few moments in boiling water.

Drain the water from the pan in which the pumpkin has been cooking and replace it with the fish stock, soy sauce, salt and mirin. Cook the pumpkin in this liquid until soft. Mix the cornflour with 2 tablespoons cold water, remove the pumpkin from the stock and stir the cornflour into the pan to thicken the liquid. Steep the prawns to stand in the thickened sauce for about 10 minutes before serving so that they can absorb the liquid.

To serve
Serve the pieces of pumpkin in a bowl and pour the sauce over them.

VEGETABLES FROM THE WOK

The wok is much more frequently used in China than Japan, but many Japanese cooks like it. In this recipe, the wok is used in the same way as a saucepan.

Method

Soak the dried mushrooms in water to cover for at least 30 minutes. Wash the savoy cabbage leaves and cut them into 4 cm/1½ in squares. Scrub the carrots and slice them into strips as thick as a finger. Wash the mangetout peas and the okra. Drain the baby corn, wipe the fresh shiitake mushrooms and wash and trim the spring onions. Slice the spring onions lengthways into thin strips.

Quickly blanch all the vegetables, except the spring onions and the dried mushrooms.

Wipe the kombu strips with a damp cloth to ensure that no grains of sand remain. Make a few cuts in the kombu and then place them in the wok. Add a little water and set over a moderate heat, removing the kombu just before the water boils.

Mix the miso with the sake, the soy sauce and the salt, add to the kombu stock. Put the blanched vegetables, plus the soaked mushrooms (including any soaking water) into the stock and cook until the vegetables are firm. Finally add in the spring onions.

To serve

Put the wok on a hot-plate to keep warm, but do not let the contents simmer. Remove the vegetables from the wok using chopsticks and place them in a bowl. Sprinkle a little sansho over them. Save the delicious stock until last.

Ingredients

150 g/6 oz dried shiitake mushrooms
200 g/7 oz savoy cabbage leaves
8 medium-sized carrots
200 g/7 oz mangetout peas
200 g/7 oz okra
200 g/7 oz canned baby corn
200 g/7 oz shiitake mushrooms
2 spring onions
10 × 10 cm/4 in kombu
180 ml/6 fl oz miso
1 teaspoon sake
1 teaspoon soy sauce
salt
1 teaspoon sansho

Overleaf:
Vegetables from the wok

TERRINE OF CHINESE LEAVES WITH SALMON

Steaming is one of the best ways to cook vegetables as the natural flavour and goodness of the food is preserved.

Ingredients

300 g/11 oz salmon fillet
6 large Chinese leaves (bok choy)
salt
1 egg
2 teaspoons oil
1 tablespoon sake
2 tablespoons soy sauce
1½ tablespoons cornflour or arrowroot
2 tablespoons mirin
300 ml/9 fl oz fish stock
1 untreated lemon

Method

Examine the salmon fillet carefully to ensure no bones remain, then cut it into slices 1 cm/½ inch thick.

Wash the Chinese leaves and discard the thick stems.

Blanch the Chinese leaves in boiling salted water for a few moments. Beat the egg. Grease a soufflé dish with the oil and line it with half the cabbage leaves. Combine 1 tablespoon of sake, 1 tablespoon of soy sauce and 1 tablespoon of the cornflour or arrowroot with the beaten egg. Divide this mixture into two equal portions and pour one half over the Chinese leaves. Carefully layer the slices of salmon over the leaves and then pour the other half of the egg mixture over the fish.

Cover the terrine with the remaining cabbage leaves. Peel the lemon thinly, ensuring that no pith adheres to the zest.

Take a large saucepan, fill it with 5 cm/2 in water and bring to the boil. As soon as the water starts to steam, place the soufflé dish in the steamer and cook for ten minutes.

Mix the mirin with the rest of the soy sauce and the fish stock and bring to the boil. Add the remaining cornflour or arrowroot and the lemon zest and bring the liquid to the boil again, stirring constantly.

Remove the lemon peel and cut it into thin strips.

To serve

Remove the terrine from the soufflé dish and cut it into four thick portions.

Arrange it on plates and pour the sauce over it. Garnish with the thin strips of lemon peel.

CHINESE LEAVES WITH SPRING RAIN NOODLES

Method

Wash the Chinese leaves and slice it into julienne strips.
Slice the pork thinly and then cut it into 5 cm/2 in strips.
Cook the noodles for about 5 minutes in plenty of boiling water. Drain them and then cut them into 10 cm/4 in lengths.

In another pan, bring the fish stock to the boil, and add the cabbage leaves, soy sauce, salt and sake. When it is boiling, add the pork slices. Skim off any foam that forms on the surface. Finally add the noodles.

To serve

When the stock has thickened, serve it in four small bowls.

Ingredients

1 head Chinese leaves
300 g/11 oz lean, boneless pork
70 g/3 oz glass or 'spring rain' noodles
1 l/1¾ pints fish stock
3 tablespoons soy sauce
1½ teaspoons salt
3 tablespoons sake

COURGETTES WITH THEIR FLOWER-HEADS

Only small, young courgettes can give this dish its special flavour.
The flower-heads give off a wonderful aroma.

Method

Wash the courgettes and the flowers.
Stone the umeboshi and sieve the flesh.
Add the rice vinegar, white wine and soy sauce. Stir well.

Pour the sauce into four small bowls and add a few drops of lemon juice to taste.

To serve

Neatly arrange the courgettes, flowers and shrimps in the sauce.

Ingredients

12 baby courgettes
12 courgette flower heads
5 umeboshi
2 tablespoons rice vinegar or apple vinegar
1 tablespoon white wine
1 teaspoon soy sauce
lemon juice
12 small cooked, peeled shrimps

SCAMPI IN OKRA SAUCE

Miyuga is a variety of pickled ginger. If it is not available, then half a teaspoon of fresh grated ginger root can be used instead.

Ingredients
4 okra
1 teaspoon wasabi
1 piece of miyuga
3 tablespoons soy sauce
12 cooked crawfish tails
1 bunch fresh dill

Method
Sprinkle the okra with salt, then blanch for a few seconds until the pods turn a beautiful deep green colour. When they have cooled, chop the pods finely.
Mix the wasabi with half a teaspoon of water and cut the miyuga into paper-thin strips.

Combine the chopped okra with the wasabi and the soy sauce.

To serve
Divide the mixture into four small bowls, each with three crayfish tails. Garnish with the strips of miyuga and the fresh dill.

AUBERGINE STEAKS

A genuine vegetarian dish despite the 'steaks'.

Ingredients
2 aubergines
salt
2 sweet red peppers
1 clove of garlic
2 tablespoons sesame paste
1 tablespoon miso
3 tablespoons mayonnaise
3 tablespoons natural yoghurt
½ tablespoon wine vinegar
freshly ground black pepper
2 tablespoons oil

Method
Wash the aubergines and cut them into slices 1½ cm/½ in thick.
Lay the slices on a dish, sprinkle with salt and leave for 15 minutes.

Dry the aubergines with a paper towel.
Wash the red peppers, seed them and slice them into strips. Leave to drain.
Peel and crush the garlic, then mix with the sesame paste, the miso, mayonnaise, yoghurt and vinegar. Salt lightly but pepper generously. Reserve the mixture

Heat the oil in a frying pan. Fry the aubergines and the peppers until they are both a crispy brown.

To serve
Place the aubergine 'steaks' and peppers on four plates and pour the sauce over them.

BAMBOO SHOOTS WITH GREEN SAUCE

Try to get canned unsliced bamboo shoots. These are of a better quality than sliced bamboo shoots. Fresh bamboo shoots naturally have the best flavour, but they are difficult to find in our shops and supermarkets.

Method
Drain the bamboo shoots, then cut them into pieces 2 cm/1 in long and 1 cm/½ inch wide. Add a tablespoon of sugar, salt, two tablespoons of sake and the kombu to the fish stock and bring to the boil quickly. As soon as it is boiling, add the bamboo shoots and stir constantly until the stock has thickened.

Wash the spinach and leave to drain. Reduce it to a paste with a pestle in a mortar.

Combine the spinach paste with 250 ml/8 fl oz water and bring to the boil. Boil rapidly for a few moments, then pass it through a sieve and drain.

Put the miso, the mirin, the rest of the sugar and the sake in a saucepan and warm through over a gentle heat stirring constantly.

When the thickened stock has cooled, add the spinach paste and stir in well until the sauce is a uniformly bright green colour.

Stir in the chili powder and then carefully add the bamboo shoots.

To serve
Leave to stand for a minute or two and then serve in four small bowls.

Ingredients
300 g/11 oz canned bamboo shoots
250 ml/8 fl oz fish stock
2 tablespoons sugar
salt
3 tablespoons sake
5 × 5 cm/2 in kombu
200 g/7 oz spinach
2 tablespoons white miso
1 tablespoon mirin
1 teaspoon ground chili powder

KOHLRABI SALAD

Ingredients
1 kg/2½ lb kohlrabi
salt
3 tablespoons vinegar
2 tablespoons sugar
10 × 10 cm/4 in kombu

Method
Wash and peel the kohlrabi and slice it thinly. Arrange the slices on a dish and sprinkle liberally with salt. Using a board smaller than the dish, cover the kohlrabi. Place a heavy weight on the board and leave the salted slices to stand for at least one hour.

Mix the vinegar with the sugar and then cut the kombu into strips 3 cm/1 in long. Remove the weight and board from the kohlrabi and then stir in the kombu and vinegar. Put the board and weight back on and leave for a further 12 hours.

To serve
Drain the salted liquid from the kohlrabi and serve in four small bowls.

JAPORE POTATOES

Ingredients
40 tiny new potatoes
8 thin slices of ham
10g/¼ oz grated ginger root
500 ml/16 fl oz fish stock
2 tablespoons sake
2 tablespoons sugar
3 tablespoons soy sauce

Method
Wash the potatoes thoroughly and leave them to drain. Slice the ham into strips 5 cm/2 in long. Peel the ginger and grate finely.

Put the potatoes in the stock, together with the ham. Cover and simmer on a moderate heat, until the potatoes are cooked.
Stir the sake, sugar and soy sauce together and heat through gently. Shake the pan occasionally to prevent burning.

To serve
Serve the potatoes on a large dish and garnish with the grated ginger.

CHICKEN BREAST WITH CELERY

For this dish, the celery is softened in the marinade. If a proper steamer is not available, then the chicken breast can be cooked in steam as described here.

Ingredients
200 g/7oz boned chicken breast
2 tablespoons coarse salt
1 tablespoon sake
180 g/7 oz celery
1 teaspoon hot prepared mustard
1 tablespoon soy sauce

Method
Rub salt into the chicken breast, sprinkle it with the sake and slice it into strips. Reserve it.
Wash the celery and discard the leaves. Place the celery stalks in salted water and leave for 3 hours. Slice the stalks into strips the size of matchsticks.

To steam the chicken, take a shallow saucepan or sauté pan and put a cup in it upside down in about 4 cm/2 inches of water. Bring the water to the boil. As soon as the water starts to steam, carefully place the plate containing the chicken on the upturned cup. Cover the saucepan with a tight-fitting lid and leave the chicken to cook for about 6 minutes. Remove the plate from the pan, taking care as it will be very hot. Leave the chicken to cool down on another plate. Tear the chicken into bite-sized pieces by hand.

Stir the mustard into the soy sauce and then combine with the celery and the chicken.

To serve
Mix everything together in a bowl. Season with soy sauce, if required.

CUCUMBER AND AUBERGINE SALAD

Aubergines are generally not suitable for eating raw; however, as long as the wafer-thin slices are well-marinated, this recipe provides an exception to the rule.

Method
Wash the cucumber and aubergines. Halve them both lengthways and then cut them into very thin slices. Put the slices in a saucepan, sprinkle with salt and mix well.
Add the shisonomi to the vegetables and stir well. Add more shisonomi if required.

Using a board smaller than the dish, cover the vegetables. Place a heavy weight, such as a 1 kg/2 lb can, on the board and leave to stand for at least one hour.

To serve
Remove the weight and drain off any liquid. Give everything a final stir, then serve in a salad bowl.

Ingredients
1 cucumber
1 aubergine
2 teaspoons salt
1 tablespoon canned shisonomi

RED PEPPERS IN SAUCE

Use large sweet red peppers for this dish, pimentos would make the taste far too strong.

Method
Halve the red peppers lengthways and discard the stems and seeds. Wash and drain.

Heat a little oil in a frying-pan and fry the peppers until they are soft. Add the soy sauce, sake and mirin and bring to the boil. As soon as the liquid starts to bubble, remove the pan from the heat and add the katsuobushi.

To serve
Make sure the peppers and katsuobushi are well mixed and then serve in four small bowls.

Ingredients
150 g/6 oz sweet red peppers
1 tablespoon oil
4 tablespoons soy sauce
3 tablespoons sake
1½ tablespoons mirin
1 pinch katsuobushi

STEAMED MUSHROOMS WITH VEGETABLES

A lot of salt and some pine needles, but no herbs or spices – the result is a dish with a wonderful aroma.

Ingredients

150 g/6 oz each of shimeji, enoki and shiitake mushrooms
150 g/6 oz Swiss chard
100 g/4 oz dandelion leaves
100 g/4 oz mangetout peas
12 canned gingko nuts
8 canned water chestnuts
1 sprig of pine needles
500 g/1 lb 2 oz coarse sea salt
125 g/5 oz white radish (daikon or mooli)
2 shallots
2 tablespoons sake
3 tablespoons soy sauce
3 tablespoons freshly squeezed lemon juice
shichimi togarashi

Method

Preheat the oven to 200°C/400F/Gas mark 6.

Wash the mushrooms and dry them thoroughly. Cut a cross in the top of the cap of the larger mushrooms. Wash the other vegetables. Remove the thick ribs from the Swiss chard and the dandelion leaves. Make a single cut in the mangetout peas from tip to stalk. Thread the gingko nuts on to four small skewers.

Drain the water chestnuts and dry them carefully.

Spread a layer of salt over the bottom of an unglazed earthenware pot about 30 cm/12 in. in diameter. Moisten the salt with a few drops of water and then warm through on the stove at a moderate heat.

Spread a thin layer of pine needles over the salt and then cover with the mushrooms, vegetables, gingko nuts and water chestnuts. Finally, scatter a few more pine needles over the vegetables. Cover the pot with a tight-fitting lid and, if necessary, use aluminium foil to help create a tight seal.

Bake the dish in the oven for about 20 minutes. Do not remove the lid or shake the pot.

Meanwhile prepare the sauce. Peel the radish and grate it finely. Cut the shallots into very thin slices. Warm the sake in a small saucepan, remove it from the stove quickly and then flambé it.

Carefully shake the pot until the flame goes out. Leave the sake in a bowl to cool and then add the radish, shallots, soy sauce, lemon juice and shichimi togarashi. Stir well.

To serve

Remove the lid, discard the pine needles and serve straight from the pot. Put some of the sake sauce in each of the four bowls. Using chopsticks, choose one of the delicately-flavoured mushrooms or other vegetable from the pot and dip it in the sake sauce.

Steamed mushrooms with vegetables

SWEET POTATO DUMPLINGS STUFFED WITH PORK

Sweet potatoes have a delicate flavour, reminiscent of chestnuts, and it gives these dumplings an inimitable taste.

Ingredients
*450 g/1 lb sweet
potatoes
2 tablespoons oil
2 tablespoons chopped
spring onions
100 g/4 oz minced pork
1 tablespoons sake
2 teaspoons soy sauce
pinch freshly-ground
green pepper
80 g/3 oz cornflour or
arrowroot
1 tablespoon sesame
seeds
a few drops of vinegar*

Method
Trim both ends of the potatoes, peel and wash. Cut the potatoes into 2 cm/1 in slices, placing them immediately in cold water, so that they do not discolour. When they are all prepared, cook them in a little water, drain and pass them through a sieve. Keep them warm.

Heat 2 teaspoons of oil in a frying pan. Fry the spring onions first and then the minced pork. Add the sake, 1 teaspoon of the soy sauce and a large pinch of green pepper.

Fry for a few minutes longer.

Carefully combine the potatoes with the cornflour or arrowroot. Divide both the minced pork mixture and the potatoes into eight portions. Take a portion of minced pork and a portion of potatoes and shape them into dumplings.

Heat up 1½ tablespoons of oil in a frying pan and fry the dumplings on all sides. This needs to be done quickly and evenly to ensure that the dumplings do not fall apart.

To serve
Sprinkle sesame seeds over the dumplings and arrange on four plates. Add vinegar and soy sauce to taste.

WHITE RADISH WITH PORK RIBS

Method

Peel the white radish. Cut it in half lengthways and then again into 2 cm/1 in lengths. Cut the radish leaves into 3 cm/1 in strips. and blanch them in boiling water for 3 minutes. Leave the mushrooms to soak in lukewarm water for 15 to 20 minutes. Drain them, squeezing out the excess water and discard the stalks.

In a deep-fryer, fry the ribs in hot oil until they are golden-brown. Add the radishes and shiitake mushrooms to the pork and continue to fry for a few more minutes. Sprinkle the sake and a little water into the deep fryer and bring to the boil.

When the liquid boils, skim off any fat and reduce the heat. Add the sugar, mirin and half of the soy sauce. Cover the pan and cook gently for 15 minutes. Then add the rest of the soy sauce and continue to cook for another 10 minutes. Finally add the radish leaves and cook for 1 more minute.

To serve

Serve in a large bowl

Ingredients

800 g/2 lb white radish with leaves
8 dried shiitake mushrooms
1 tablespoon oil
600 g/1 lb short pork ribs
3 tablespoons sake
2 tablespoons mirin
1 tablespoon sugar
5 tablespoons soy sauce

SHIITAKE MUSHROOMS WITH LIME SAUCE

Method

Wash the mushrooms, remove the stalks and sprinkle the caps with salt. Fry the mushrooms on both sides over a moderate heat. Remove the mushrooms from the frying-pan and slice them thinly.

Bring some salted water to the boil and cook the turnip leaves until tender. Drain and cut into 3 cm/1 in lengths.

Squeeze the juice from the limes and mix it with the fish stock and the soy sauce.

Mix together the mushrooms, turnip leaves and sauce.

To serve

Serve in four small bowls.

Ingredients

12 fresh shiitake mushrooms
salt
100 g/4 oz spring turnip leaves
4 limes
2 tablespoons fish stock
2 tablespoons soy sauce

PASTA & RICE

SUSHI, RICE AND NOODLES

How to Make Tasty Titbits from Rice

Small they may be, possibly only a mouthful, but Japanese cuisine would be incomplete without them. They are, of course, sushi. These delectable morsels look so inviting, but they are by no means so easy to make.

It is worth practising the art of rolling and shaping sushi as it is a difficult skill to master. The nori leaf might be too small for the filling, there might not be enough rice, or the filling might not be in the middle. The condition of the rice when cooked is also very important. It must not be too hard or too soft. Rice cooked for sushi should be mixed with rice vinegar in a wooden tub. The wood can thus absorb any excess moisture from the rice.

It is also very important that all the ingredients are at the same temperature, that is to say, room temperature. To roll sushi correctly, a special bamboo mat is required. This should be laid out on the work surface with the nori on top. The taste of the nori is enhanced if the outside of the leaf is first toasted over a hot flame. The nori is positioned so that a strip of the mat furthest from the body is left empty. The rice must then be spread evenly over the nori, taking care not to crush the grains.

Are all the other ingredients completely dry? That is another important factor. Make a furrow in the middle of the rice and spread the filling into it. Now roll up the bamboo mat, so that the nori wraps round the rice.

The sushi roll should be firm, with the rice and filling not yielding when pressed.

Moisten the edges of the nori and join them together. Remove the bamboo mat. Place the sushi roll on a chopping board, seam downwards. Have ready a bowl of ice water to which a few drops of rice vinegar have been added. Dip a smooth, very sharp knife in the cold, vinegared water and slice the roll into six or eight pieces. If sushi rolls look too difficult for the home cook, then nigiri-sushi should prove less daunting. A small ball of rice is shaped in one hand and the coating, usually raw fish, held in the other. The fish is then wrapped round the rice, with possibly a little wasabi horseradish dabbed on the fish. This delicious morsel is now ready to eat.

Rice

The Japanese use two main types of rice:

Uruchi Rice is translucent and is the type of rice best suited for sushi, but is also a good rice for eating with vegetables. Genuine uruchi rice is not available in Europe, but American short-grained rice is a close substitute.

Mochi Rice or glutinous rice is an opaque white rice, which is round-grained and sticky. It is used mainly for chimaki and sekihan.

In the following recipes, 'rice' refers to **Uruchi Rice**. If **Mochi Rice** is required, it will be specified.

Noodles

At first sight, there seems to be a wide

choice of noodles on offer, but, in actual fact, they are just variations of a few main types.

Harusame, Glass or Spring Rain Noodles are made from potato starch. When cooked they are said to resemble the thin transparent streaks of a gentle spring rain. Hence the romantic name of harusame, which means spring rain. Depending on the particular shape, glass noodles can be scalded very quickly in hot, vinegared water or else just dipped in boiling water. In both cases, the noodles become transparent, but they should not be cooked for too long, as they can very easily dissolve.

Soba or Buckwheat Noodles are made from buckwheat, a dark pyramid-shaped grain, salt and water. Sometimes grated yam (a tropical root with a high starch content) is added as a binding agent. Soba noodles are sold fresh, pre-cooked or dried. To get the right 'firmness', put them in cold water, bring to the boil and then plunge them into cold water. Repeat this process twice.

Somen are fine durum wheat noodles that are made from flour, water and salt. Thick lengths of noodle dough are coated with oil and drawn out into paper-thin threads. These are then dried and cut into smaller lengths. Sometimes the dough is coloured with tea.

Udon are thick durum wheat wheat noodles are made from flour, water and salt. Although they are not as firm as spaghetti, they must still be cooked 'al dente'. They come in several shapes and sizes and can be purchased fresh, pre-cooked or dried.

With the exception of the glass noodles, Japanese noodles taste saltier than European noodles and pasta. They are usually sold neatly packaged, perhaps in small bundles tied in the middle. There may be different types in one pack and some may be coloured with natural colourings. They are often used to make attractive displays in the shops.

To cook rice

Rice has the same significance in Japanese life as bread does in the West. It will normally be placed in a bowl on the table and eaten as an accompaniment to other dishes.
As a general rule, when cooking rice, the ratio of rice to water should be in the region of 1:1.2.

Ingredients
200 g/7 oz uruchi rice (Japanese short-grained rice)
375 ml/13 fl oz water

Method
Place the rice in a sieve and wash it several waters until the water remains clear. Leave the rice to drain for 1 hour.
Put the required quantity of cooking water in a large saucepan with the rice and leave it to soak for about 30 minutes.
Bring the rice to the boil over a moderate heat, stirring occasionally, so that the rice does not stick. When it is boiling, cover and leave to simmer for a further ten minutes, until all the water has been absorbed. Reduce the heat as far as possible and leave the rice to stand for about 5 minutes. Then remove the lid.
Serve the rice hot.

Home-made noodles

This is a basic recipe for home-made noodles which are particularly tasty in soup or sukiyaki.

Ingredients
400 g/14 oz strong, plain unbleached flour
1 tablespoon salt
250 ml/8 fl oz water

Method
Sift the flour and dissolve the salt in the water.
Mix a little of the water with the flour and stir well. Repeat the process until all the water has been used up.
Knead the dough well until it is smooth. Wrap it in a damp cloth and leave it to rest for 30 minutes.
Lightly flour a pastry board and knead the dough again briefly with both hands.
Press the dough flat with the heel of the hand, fold back and then press down again. Continue kneading until the dough has an elastic texture.
Sprinkle more flour on the board and roll the dough to an even thickness of 5 mm/¼ inch, working out from the middle.
Fold the dough into a strip 5 cm/2 in wide. Cut across the strip with a sharp knife to make ribbons 5 mm/¼ inch wide. Pick up the noodles and carefully shake off the excess flour. They can then be cooked immediately or left to dry and stored.

To cook sushi rice

Sushi chefs use uruchi rice. It is stickier than long-grained rice nor can it be cooked like Italian short-grained rice. Sushi rice requires 10% less water. The correct ratio of rice to water should be 1:1.1. The missing 10% is replaced by a mixture of vinegar, sugar and salt.

To cook sushi rice the following proportions of rice, water, vinegar, sugar and salt are recommended:

Rice	Water	Vinegar	Sugar	Salt
200 g/7 oz	270 ml/9 fl oz	20 ml/1 tbsp	½ tbsp	½ teaspoon
300g/11 oz	400 ml/8 fl oz	30 ml/2 tbsp	¾ tbsp	¾ teaspoon
400 g/14 oz	540 ml/17 fl oz	40 ml/2½ tbsp	1 tbsp	1 teaspoon

Method

Take a large saucepan and bring the rice vinegar, sugar, salt and mirin to the boil uncovered. As soon as it comes to the boil, remove the pan from the heat and leave the contents to cool to room temperature.

Wash the rice until the water runs clear and then leave it to drain for 1 hour. Put the rice and the kombu in a saucepan with 500 ml/16 fl oz water. Stirring constantly, bring it to the boil quickly. Then reduce the heat, cover and simmer for ten minutes, or until the rice has absorbed all the liquid. Keep warm at a gentle heat for 5 more minutes, then remove from the heat altogether and leave for a further 5 minutes. Uncover and remove the kombu.

Spoon the rice into an unvarnished wooden bowl and combine with the hot rice vinegar sauce. To allow any surplus liquid to evaporate, the rice should be stirred and fanned. This will also help to cool the rice.

To use

This rice can be used in any sushi recipe.

Ingredients

3 tablespoons rice vinegar
1 tablespoon sugar
1 teaspoon salt
1½ tablespoons mirin
400 g/14 oz uruchi rice (Japanese short-grained rice)
5 × 5 cm/2 in kombu

Assorted rice balls

Rice balls are one of Japan's favourite foods. They are the bread-and-butter of Japanese fare and they come in many different variations. Only a small selection can be offered here.

Ingredients
*About 2½ lb uruchi rice
(5 × 250 ml/8 fl oz cups)
1.5 l/24 fl oz water*

Variation 1
*100 g/4 oz salmon fillet
1 untreated lemon
1 tablespoon aonori*

Variation 2
*100 g/4 oz cod roe
2 tablespoons black
sesame seeds
1 tablespoon umeboshi*

For the Rice
Cook the rice according to the instructions given on page 70 and keep it warm, so that it will stick better. Cooled rice does not stick together so well.

Have ready a bowl of ice water and a dish of salt. The water is for keeping the hands moist and the salt for coating the palm of the hand. The rice balls must always be shaped quickly and carefully. Eight 250-ml/8-oz cups of cooked rice are sufficient to make 15 rice balls.

I. Rice balls with salmon
Grill the salmon under a hot grill. Leave to cool and then cut into tiny pieces.
Cut the lemon into paper-thin slices.
Take a handful of rice, make a hole in the centre with a finger and fill it with salmon morsels. Use both hands to shape the rice into a small ball. Sprinkle it with the aonori and garnish with the lemon slices. Repeat this process 3 or 4 times.

II. Rice balls with Cod Roe and Sesame Seeds
Cook the cod roe quickly under a hot grill, then crumble it so that it resembles poppy seeds. Toast the sesame seeds in a dry frying pan and leave to cool.
As with the salmon rice balls above, shape the rice into a small ball with the cod roe. Coat with sesame seed and then place a little umeboshi on the top.

To serve
Whether there is just one type of rice ball on offer or a variety, they must always be arranged attractively on a serving platter.

It is also the custom to serve them with a bowl of pickled ginger on the side. Ginger neutralises and refreshes the taste buds.

*Assorted
rice balls*

ASSORTED RICE BALLS

The filling for the rice balls does not always have to be fish, as the following variations prove.

Rice

Ingredients
*About 2½ lb uruchi rice
(5 × 250 ml/8 fl oz cups)
1½ l/24 fl oz water*

*Variation 3
100 g/4 oz pickled white
radish
2 tablespoons soy sauce
3 tablespoons
katsuobushi
10 × 10 cm/4 in
ajitsukenori*

*Variation 4
100 g/4 oz red kidney
beans, soaked in water
to cover for at least
2 hours
50 g/2 oz canned sweet
chestnuts
1 tablespoon sugar*

*Variation 5
1 leek
50 g/2 oz ready cooked
shrimps
pickled ginger*

For the Rice
Cook the rice according to the instructions given on page 70 and keep it warm, so that it will stick better. Cooled rice does not stick together so well.

Have ready a bowl of ice water and a dish of salt. The water is for keeping the hands moist and the salt for coating the palm of the hand. The rice balls must always be shaped quickly and carefully. Eight 250-ml/8-oz cups of cooked rice are sufficient to make 15 rice balls.

III. Rice Balls with Pickled Radish and Katsuobushi
Take 50 g/2 oz of pickled radish, chop finely and mix with a little soy sauce. Follow the instructions for variation I and quickly shape the balls of rice with the katsuobushi. Cut the ajitsukenori into strips 1 cm/½ inch wide and 10 cm/4 in long. Wrap the strips around the middle of the rice balls and cover the remaining surface area with chopped radish.

IV. Rice Balls with Red Beans and Chestnuts
Cook the beans in plenty of water for about 1 hour. Drain the chestnuts and cut into small pieces. Mix the beans and chestnuts and add the sugar. As in variation I, shape the rice balls and fill them with the bean-and-chestnut mixture.

V. Rice Balls with Leek and Shrimps
Chop the leek into very thin strips and blanch quickly in hot water. Halve the shrimps and chop finely. Shape the balls with the rice, leek and shrimps according to the instructions in variation I.

To serve
Serve as described on page 72.

SQUID STUFFED WITH RICE

If the ink sac is still inside the squid, then it can be added to the rice.

Method

Wash the rice and leave to soak overnight. Drain thoroughly.

Wash the squid. Cut off the tentacles and chop them into 5 cm/2 in lengths.

Leave the dried shrimps and mushroom to soak for 30 minutes in a little warm water. Drain, reserving 1 tablespoon of the water.

Dice the pork, bamboo shoots, mushroom and shrimps into 5 mm/ ¼ inch cubes.

Heat the oil in a saucepan and fry the tentacles with the pork, bamboo shoots, mushroom and shrimps. Add the rice and 3 tablespoons of stock, 1 tablespoon of sake, the sugar and 1 tablespoon of soy sauce. Simmer until the liquid has nearly boiled dry.

Stuff the squid loosely with the filling and close each one with a toothpick.

Put the rest of the stock into a saucepan with 1 tablespoon of the water used for soaking the shrimps and mushroom. Add the rest of the sake, mirin and 2 tablespoons of soy sauce. Place the stuffed squid in the saucepan, cover and bring quickly to the boil. As soon as it is boiling, reduce the heat and simmer gently for a further 8 minutes. Remove from the heat, uncover the pan and leave for 6 minutes, until the squid skins are glossy.

To serve

Cut the squid into thick slices and serve on four plates.

Ingredients

200 g/7 oz mochi
(glutinous) rice
4 small whole squid
10g/½ oz dried shrimps
1 dried shiitake
mushroom
30 g/1 oz lean pork
20 g/½ oz canned
bamboo shoots
2 teaspoons vegetable
oil
250 ml/8 fl oz chicken
stock
80 ml/3 fl oz sake
½ teaspoon sugar
3 tablespoons soy sauce
80 ml/3 fl oz mirin

STEAMED RICE WITH GINGKO NUTS AND MUSHROOMS

Two types of rice are recommended for this recipe, mochi rice and uruchi rice. For a delicate fragrance, add a pine twig.

Ingredients
100 g/4 oz chicken breast
1 carrot
40g/1½ oz fresh shiitake mushrooms
40g/1½ oz oyster mushrooms
40g/1½ oz ceps
3 tablespoons soy sauce
1 tablespoon sake
1 tablespoon mirin
250 g/8 oz mochi (glutinous) rice
500 g/1 lb uruchi rice
25 canned gingko nuts
720 ml/18 fl oz fish stock
16 ready-to-use marinated vine leaves
a few chives

Method
Dice the chicken breast into 5 mm/¼ in cubes.
Peel the carrot and dice it into cubes of the same size.
Wash all the mushrooms and drain them. Slice them into wafer-thin strips.
Let the soy sauce, sake, mirin, chicken, carrots and mushrooms soak together in a bowl for 10 minutes.

Put all the ingredients, including the gingko nuts and the stock, into a large saucepan and boil over a moderate heat until the sauce has reduced by half and the rice is cooked.
Put a portion of the rice mixture into two vine leaves and fold into parcels.
Tie up each parcel with a length of chives.
Place the vine leaf parcels in a steamer and cook for 15 minutes.

To serve
Arrange the little parcels on four plates. If you are using an attractive bamboo steamer, the parcels can be brought to the table in the bamboo basket.

Steamed Rice with Gingko Nuts and Mushrooms

CHAKIN SUSHI

This type of sushi differs from the others in that thin slices of pancake are used to hold the rice together instead of nori leaf.

Ingredients
375 g/12 oz uruchi rice
3 dried shiitake
mushrooms
2 tablespoons sesame
seeds
2 tablespoons cornflour
4 eggs
5 tablespoons sugar
salt
oil for frying
30 g/1 oz dried gourd
cut into strips
350 ml/12 fl oz fish
stock
2½ tablespoons soy
sauce
1 tablespoon mirin
1½ nori leaves
200 g/7 oz fresh
shrimps
1 tablespoon sake
a little red food
colouring

Method
Prepare the rice according to the recipe on page 71 and reserve. Soak the shiitake mushrooms in warm water for about 20 minutes. Toast the sesame seeds in a dry frying-pan and then crush them to release the full aroma. Stir the cornflour into 1 tablespoon water and then add the eggs, 2 tablespoons sugar and a pinch of salt. Mix well. Heat a dry omelette pan, add a few drops of oil and heat. Make eight small, thin pancakes from the mixture.

Rub a little salt into the gourd strips, rinse and then place in boiling water for five minutes. Remove the mushrooms from the water and discard the stalks.

Put the fish stock, a little salt, soy sauce, 3 tablespoons sugar and the mirin in a saucepan. Add the gourd strips and mushrooms and boil at a moderate heat. Then remove the gourd strips and mushrooms. Reserve half of the gourd strips for use later to use as ribbons and chop the other half finely with the mushrooms.

Toast one side of the nori leaves in a frying-pan without oil and then crumble them.

Reserve some of the shrimps for the garnish. Purée the remainder, along with a little salt, the sugar, the sake and the red food colouring.

Mix the rice vinegar with the gourd and mushrooms and add the toasted sesame seeds and the crumbled nori. Divide the rice into 8 equal-sized balls.

Lay the pancakes on a board and put a ball of rice in the middle of each one. Carefully fold the edges of each pancake over the filling to enclose it as you would if making sushi with nori. Use a strip of gourd as a ribbon to tie the pancake together, leaving it open at one end.

To serve
Arrange neatly on a serving dish or a large plate. Place a small shrimp in the open end of the pancake.

RAPESEED FLOWER SUSHI

This dish is often prepared at the time of the Cherry Blossom Festival.
The rice is garnished with 'rapeseed flowers' made from radish.

Method

Cut the radish into 5 cm/2 in cubes. Wash the shiso leaves and the lime and then cut both into thin slices

Toast one side of the nori leaf in a frying pan without oil and then cut it into narrow strips with scissors. Toast the sesame seeds in a frying pan without fat.

Wash the rice and drain it. Put it in a saucepan with 750 ml/12 fl oz cold water and leave to soak for 30 minutes.

Bring the rice vinegar, sugar, salt and sake to the boil. As soon as the liquid boils, remove the pan from the heat and leave to cool.

Add the kombu to the rice, cover and bring to the boil over a moderate heat. As soon as the rice begins to boil, remove the kombu, cover the pan again and boil for a further 10 minutes, until all the water has been absorbed. Keep the rice warm and leave to stand for 5 minutes without stirring.

Spoon the rice into wooden bowl and quickly stir the rice vinegar mixture into it with a wooden rice spoon. Continue to stir and fan the rice for about 10 minutes. Cover the dish with a clean cloth and leave to cool to room temperature. As soon as it has cooled, gently stir in the sesame seeds and lime peel.

To serve

Arrange the rice on four plates and sprinkle with the nori. Garnish the rice with rape seed 'flowers' cut from the radish and the shiso leaves.

Ingredients

1 pickled white radish about 10 cm/4 in long
8 shiso leaves
1 untreated lime
1 nori leaf
4 tablespoons sesame seeds
80 ml/3 fl oz rice vinegar
1 teaspoon sugar
salt
1 tablespoon sake
3 cups uruchi rice (Japanese short-grain rice)
15 × 15-cm/6-in pieces kombu

MAKIZUSHI

Rice, mushrooms and strips of gourd form the filling for this sushi roll. It is then wrapped in a nori leaf.

Ingredients
*500 g/16 oz uruchi rice
(Japanese short-grained
rice)
6 dried shiitake
mushrooms
4 tablespoons soy sauce
4 tablespoons sugar
30 g/1 oz dried gourd
strips
3 nori leaves
3 eggs
salt
oil
10 spring turnip stalks
1 medium-sized carrot*

Method
Prepare the rice according to the recipe on page 71 and reserve it. Soak the shiitake mushrooms in warm water for about 20 minutes. Drain the mushrooms, reserving the liquid, and cut off their stems. Cut the caps into thin strips, then cook them in the reserved water, with 3 tablespoons of soy sauce and 3 tablespoons of the sugar.

Rub salt into the dried gourd strips, blanch them quickly in boiling water and then rinse. Add the rest of the soy sauce, the rinsed gourd strips and a add little more water to the mushrooms. Continue to simmer.

Toast one side of the nori leaves in a dry frying-pan.

Beat the eggs with the rest of the sugar and a little salt. Pour a third of the beaten egg into a small, lightly oiled frying-pan to make a sweet omelette. Make two more omelettes with the rest of the egg mixture, and cut them to roughly the same size as the nori leaves. Wash the turnip stalks, peel the carrots and cut them into julienne strips. Blanch both the vegetables quickly in boiling, salted water.

Lay a bamboo mat covered with a piece of clingfilm on the work surface and place one of the nori leaves on it. Put one of the omelettes on top but, on the side furthest away from you, leave 1 cm/½ in strip of the nori leaf free. Put half the rice on the omelette and then add the mushrooms, gourd, turnip stalks and julienned carrots in a strip along the middle. Moisten the exposed strip of nori with a little vinegar. Hold the ingredients in place with the fingers and roll up firmly, using both thumbs to roll up the bamboo mat and clingfilm, rather like making a Swiss roll. Repeat the process for the second and third nori leaf, using up the rest of the ingredients.

To serve
Cut each roll into six to eight slices and arrange them neatly on a dish or large plate.

SUSHI REINS

The diagonal patterns on these sushi are similar to the beautiful reins used by the Samurai warriors which were plaited from pieces of coloured silk.

Method

Prepare the rice according to the recipe on page 71 and reserve it. Clean the spinach and peel the carrot. Cut both into strips and blanch for a short time in boiling water.

Shell and devein the prawns, then cut off their tails. Place the prawns lengthways on skewers so that they remain straight while they are being cooked. Blanch them in boiling water and cut them in half lengthways.

Remove the skin from the eel, fillet it and poach in boiling water. Cut it into strips about 5 cm/2 in long, 3 cm/1 in wide and 2 mm/⅛ in thick.

Beat the eggs in a bowl, mixing in 2 teaspoons of sugar and a little salt. Pass the mixture through a sieve.

Heat a little oil in a frying-pan. Pour a third of the egg mixture into the pan, tipping the pan so that the egg evenly covers the base. Leave it to thicken over a low heat, shaking the pan occasionally to prevent it sticking. Flip it over.

Slide the omelette from the pan on to a board, fold it over twice and cut into strips about 2 mm/⅛ in thick. Repeat this process twice more with the remaining egg mixture.

Spread a bamboo mat on the work surface and cover with a piece of clingfilm about 25 cm/10 in square. Carefully arrange the prawns, omelette, carrot and eel in a colourful pattern of diagonal stripes.

Shape a portion of the rice into a roll about 20 cm/8 in long and lay this on top of the other ingredients.

Now take the bamboo mat and clingfilm and roll up the mat like a Swiss roll, pressing down firmly at the last stage. Then remove the sushi roll. Make two more rolls from the remaining rice and other ingredients.

To serve

Using a sharp knife, cut the prepared sushi rolls into six pieces.
Serve garnished on a dish or a serving dish.

Ingredients

4 cups mochi rice
8 spinach leaves
1 carrot
6 raw prawns
1 10 cm/4 in piece of eel
2 eggs
2 teaspoons sugar
oil
salt

Overleaf:
An assortment of Sushi

CHIRASHIZUSHI

Literally translated, chirashi means 'scattered'. These sushi are so called because several ingredients are added to or scattered over the rice.

Ingredients
*3 cups uruchi rice
(Japanese short-grained
rice)
2 dried shiitake
mushrooms
1 strip dried gourd
salt
2 tablespoons soy sauce
3 tablespoons sugar
1 tablespoon mirin
30 g/1 oz mangetout
peas
1 small carrot
8 shrimps
1 slice of tinned lotus
root (about as thick as
your thumb)
2 eggs*

Method
Prepare the rice according to the recipe on page 71 and reserve.
Allow the shiitake mushrooms to soak in warm water for about 20 minutes. Drain and reserve the water. Remove the stems and cut the caps into thin slices. Cook these in the reserved water.
Rub the dried gourd with a little salt and wash thoroughly. Add this to the mushrooms with the soy sauce and 1 tablespoon each of sugar and mirin. Allow the ingredients to cook until they are almost done, about 5 minutes.
Wash the mangetout peas and peel the carrot. Cut both into thin strips and blanch quickly in boiling water.
Shell and devein the shrimps, removing their tails. Place the shrimps on skewers and cook for 5 minutes in a saucepan of boiling water.
Drain the lotus root; cut it into very thin slices and again into quarters.
Beat the eggs, the remaining sugar and a little salt. Use this mixture to make three very thin omelettes. Be sparing with the oil when frying.
Fold the omelettes over several times and cut into thin strips.

To serve
Scatter the mushrooms, gourd and quarters of lotus root over the cooled rice and arrange the mixture into a large, shallow bowl.

STEAMED SALMON SUSHI

Yet another variety of sushi, but these are wrapped in spinach leaves and resemble little wigwams. For successful results, a lot of care is needed in the preparation.

Method

Prepare the rice according to the recipe on page 71. Add the vinegar and 3 teaspoons of the sugar and reserve. Steep the shiitake mushrooms in warm water for about 20 minutes. Rub the gourd strips with a little salt and cook gently for about 4 minutes in boiling water.

Grill the salmon on both sides for six to eight minutes and then break it by hand into small pieces.

Allow the lotus root to drain well and cut into thin slices, then cut these slices into thin strips.

Blanch the spinach leaves and the mangetout peas quickly in boiling water.

Remove the mushrooms from the water, discard the stems and chop the caps finely.

Beat the eggs with a little salt and the rest of the sugar and make three paper-thin omelettes with the minimum of oil. Fold the omelettes over several times and cut into very thin strips.

Divide the rice into eight portions and add a mixture of salmon, mushrooms, lotus root and finely-sliced mangetout peas to each portion. Lay the spinach leaves out in piles of two or three leaves. Spread the omelette strips and rice mixture evenly over all the leaves. Then roll the spinach leaves into cone-shapes so that the stems of the leaves point upwards. Wrap some gourd strips around each cone so that it resembles a small wigwam.

Place the spinach rolls in a steamer over 2-3 cm/1 in of water and steam on a high heat for about 15 minutes, making sure that the wigwams do not come into contact with the water.

To serve

Serve the rolls on an oval dish in groups of three or four. The presentation of these sushi is enhanced if they can be garnished with little canoes carved from pieces of white radish.

Ingredients

2 cups uruchi rice (Japanese short grain rice)
3 tablespoons vinegar
5 teaspoons sugar
1 teaspoon salt
2 dried shiitake mushrooms
30 g/1 oz dried gourd strips
2 slices fresh salmon about 5 cm/2 in pickled lotus root
about 16 spinach leaves
6 mangetout peas
2 eggs

MIXED SUSHI

Ingredients

500 g/1lb 2oz uruchi rice (Japanese short grain rice)
670 ml/22 fl oz water
3 tablespoons vinegar
30 g/1 oz sugar
1 teaspoon salt
3 raw prawns
1 nori leaf
1 teaspoon powdered wasabi
120 g/5 oz raw salmon
2 tablespoons salmon roe
pickled ginger

Method

Prepare the rice according to the recipe for sushi rice on page 71 and reserve. Cook the prawns in their shells for 5 minutes. Devein them, removing all but the tail of the prawns from their shells. Make the tails into rings, holding them in place with toothpicks until required. Slice the raw salmon very thinly.

Toast one side of the nori leaf in dry frying-pan and then cut it into slices 2 cm/1 in thick. Using slightly moistened hands, mould the rice into small oval balls. The quantity of rice should be sufficient for about 16 sushis.

Mix the wasabi with a little water to make a smooth paste.

Prepare the sushis in sets of four, using different ingredients for each. Cover half of them with the prawns and the other half with the sliced salmon. Spread the wasabi over 10 of them and cover the rest with the fried nori leaf strips and the salmon roe.

To serve

Present the sushi attractively on a platter and serve with the pickled ginger.

PARENTS AND CHILDREN RICE BOWL – VERSION I

In this dish the family gathered together on the rice are salmon (the parents) and salmon roe (the children).

Ingredients

300 g/11 oz uruchi rice (Japanese short grain rice)
430 ml/15 fl oz water
4 shiso leaves
300 g/11 oz fresh salmon
250 ml/8 fl oz fish stock
4 tablespoons sake
2 tablespoons mirin
salt
2 teaspoons soy sauce
6 tablespoons salmon roe

Method

Cook the rice according to the recipe on page 70. Wash the shiso leaves carefully and chop them finely.

Bring the fish stock to the boil in a pot with the sake, mirin, salt and soy sauce. Poach the salmon for a few minutes in this stock. Then remove the skin, fillet the salmon and divide into bite-sized portions. The stock can be used for another dish. While the rice is still warm, add the salmon and carefully fold in the chopped shiso leaves.

To serve

Distribute the rice and salmon mixture between four bowls. Dot each bowl with a little salmon roe.

PARENTS AND CHILDREN RICE BOWL – VERSION II

In this version, the chicken represents the parents and the egg the children.

Method

Prepare the rice according to the recipe on page 70. Cut the chicken breast into 1-cm/½- in cubes. Wash the chives and cut into 3 cm/1 in lengths.

Toast the nori leaf lightly on one side, in a dry frying-pan, and cut it into very thin strips.

Bring the fish stock to the boil in a saucepan with the soy sauce and sugar. Dissolve the cornflour or arrowroot in 2 tablespoons water, and add to the stock. Cook, stirring occasionally, until the stock starts to thicken.

Cook the cubes of chicken meat for a short time in the thickened stock. Meanwhile combine the eggs, the egg yolks and salt and mix well. Heat the oil in a pot and add a third of the egg mixture, cover and allow it to become partially solidified. Now add a further third of the egg mixture, mixing well with the egg solids already in the pot, cover and again allow to become partly solidified. Now add the chives and the final third of the egg mixture. Mix well once more, cover, remove the pan from the heat and again allow the whole mixture to solidify partially.

To serve

Divide the rice between four bowls while it is still hot. Then add the partly-solidified egg mixture, the cubes of chicken meat and the sauce. Garnish the middle of each bowl with the nori. Sprinkle with a little konasansho, if required.

Ingredients

300g/11oz uruchi rice (Japanese short grain rice)
430ml/7 fl oz water
250 g/9 oz chicken breast
1 bunch chives
1 nori leaf
400 ml/14 fl oz fish stock
4 tablespoons soy sauce
3 tablespoons sugar
1 teaspoon cornflour or arrowroot
6 eggs
3 egg yolks
1 teaspoon salt
2 teaspoons oil
a little konasansho (optional)

Summer noodles

In this refreshing dish the noodles swimming in iced water and the ice cubes are guaranteed to revive flagging spirits on a hot summer's day.

Ingredients

300 g/11 oz somen (buckwheat noodles)
200 g/7 oz chicken breast
salt
1 piece of cucumber (about 5 cm/2 in)
1 piece of leek (about 10 cm/4 in)
8 shiso leaves
5 tablespoons sake
3 tablespoons mirin
3 tablespoons soy sauce
250 ml/8 fl oz fish stock
2 tablespoons katsuobushi
ice cubes

Method

Cook the noodles in 2 l/3½ pints of water until soft. Drain in a colander and run cold water over them.

Cut the chicken fillet into bite-sized pieces, salt lightly and leave to stand for 30 minutes.

Peel the cucumber and wash the leek. Cut both into very thin strips, about 8 cm/3 in long.

Wash the shiso leaves and cut into 2 mm/1/8 in strips.

Place a cup upside down in the bottom of a saucepan. Put a plate on top and fill the pan with about 3 cm/1 in of water. Lay the chicken breast on the plate and sprinkle with sake. Cover and steam for about 15 minutes. Heat the mirin very gently in a saucepan until it is lukewarm. Remove it from the heat and flambé it. Then gently shake the pan back and forth until the flames are extinguished.

Add the soy sauce, fish stock and katsuobushi. Bring to the boil rapidly, then strain the mixture through a fine sieve.

To serve

The noodles should be served in a bowl of ice-cold water with ice cubes floating in it.

As soon as the meat has cooled down, divide it between four bowls with the cucumber, the leek and the shiso leaves. These bowls are served alongside the noodles.

Once the strained sauce has cooled to room temperature, it should be divided up in the same way and served with the noodles.

HOT NOODLE SOUP WITH DUCK

The delicate and extremely tender flesh of duck breast fillets is used in this soup.

Ingredients
1 bunch spring onions
250 g/9 oz duck breast fillets
10 × 10 cm/4 in kombu
20 g/1 oz katsuobushi
2 teaspoons light soy sauce
2 tablespoons mirin
200 g/7 oz home-made noodles (see recipe page 70)
shichimi togarashi

Method
Clean the spring onions and cut them diagonally into pieces 5 cm/ 2 in long.
Cut the duck breast fillet into strips 5 cm/2 in long and 5 mm/¼ inch wide.
Cut the kombu into four strips.
Warm four bowls in hot water.

Combine the kombu, katsuobushi, soy sauce, mirin and the water. Let this stock come briefly to the boil and then immediately strain it through a sieve lined with a tea towel or cheesecloth into another saucepan.

Bring the strained stock to the boil a second time. Add the breast fillet strips and cook briefly in the stock.

Bring a generous quantity of water to the boil and cook the home-made noodles in this. Carefully separate out the strands of noodles. As soon as the water comes to the boil, add 250 ml/8 fl oz cold water. Repeat this process three times. When the noodles are cooked, drain them in a colander and reserve a small quantity of the water. Then run cold water over the noodles until the water runs clear.

To serve
Place the noodles and fillets of duck in a bowl. Pour over the stock.
Finally, garnish with the spring onions and a little shichimi togarashi.

COLD BUCKWHEAT NOODLES WITH TEMPURA

It is important to keep the tempura dough as cold as possible. The bowl for dough should be kept on ice. On a hot summer's day, chilled noodles with hot tempura is a special treat.

Method

Shell the prawns, leaving the tail part intact, and devein carefully. Wash the shiso leaves and drain them well. Make several incisions in the kombu. Clean the spring onion and slice it into thin rings. Add 1 teaspoon of water to the powdered wasabi and mix thoroughly. Toast the nori leaf on one side without using any fat. Then crush it into fine pieces in a tea towel.

To make the sauce, bring the mirin to the boil in a saucepan. Add about 250 ml/8 fl oz water, the soy sauce, sugar, kombu and katsuobushi and bring the mixture to the boil. Remove the kombu as soon as the first bubbles appear. Over a low heat, reduce the liquid by just under a quarter. Strain it through a muslin-lined sieve. Leave to cool before dividing it between four bowls. Chill them in the refrigerator.

Put the buckwheat noodles into a large pan of boiling water. As soon as the water starts to boil, add 250 ml/8 fl oz of cold water. Repeat this process three times, until the noodles are done. They should still be 'al dente' or like spaghetti when cooked. Drain the noodles and rinse them under the cold tap until the water runs clear. Drain again thoroughly, then divide them between four bamboo plates.

Heat the oil in a deep-frier or wok until a 2.5 cm/1 in cube of bread will brown in 60 seconds. While the oil is heating, prepare the batter. Mix the egg yolk with the iced water and gradually stir in the flour. The batter should remain fairly thin and liquid, so that it drops easily off a spoon. Stand the bowl of batter in ice cubes or iced water. Now dip the shiso leaves and the prawns first into the batter, then into the hot oil. While frying them, keep the oil free of scraps of burnt batter.

To serve

Place the deep-fried prawns and shiso leaves on a plate lined with rice paper and serve them with the noodles. Pour the sauce into smaller bowls and season with the wasabi and spring onions. Sprinkle chopped nori over the noodles. Before eating the noodles and tempura, dip them into the sauce.

Ingredients

8 prawns
4 shiso leaves
10 × 10 cm/4 in kombu
1 small spring onion
1 tablespoon powdered wasabi
20 × 20 cm/8 in nori leaf
3 tablespoons mirin
5 tablespoons soy sauce
1 tablespoon sugar
5g/⅓ oz katsuobushi
250 g/9 oz soba (buckwheat noodles)
oil for frying
1 egg yolk
500ml/16 fl oz iced water
250 g/9 oz flour

MEAT

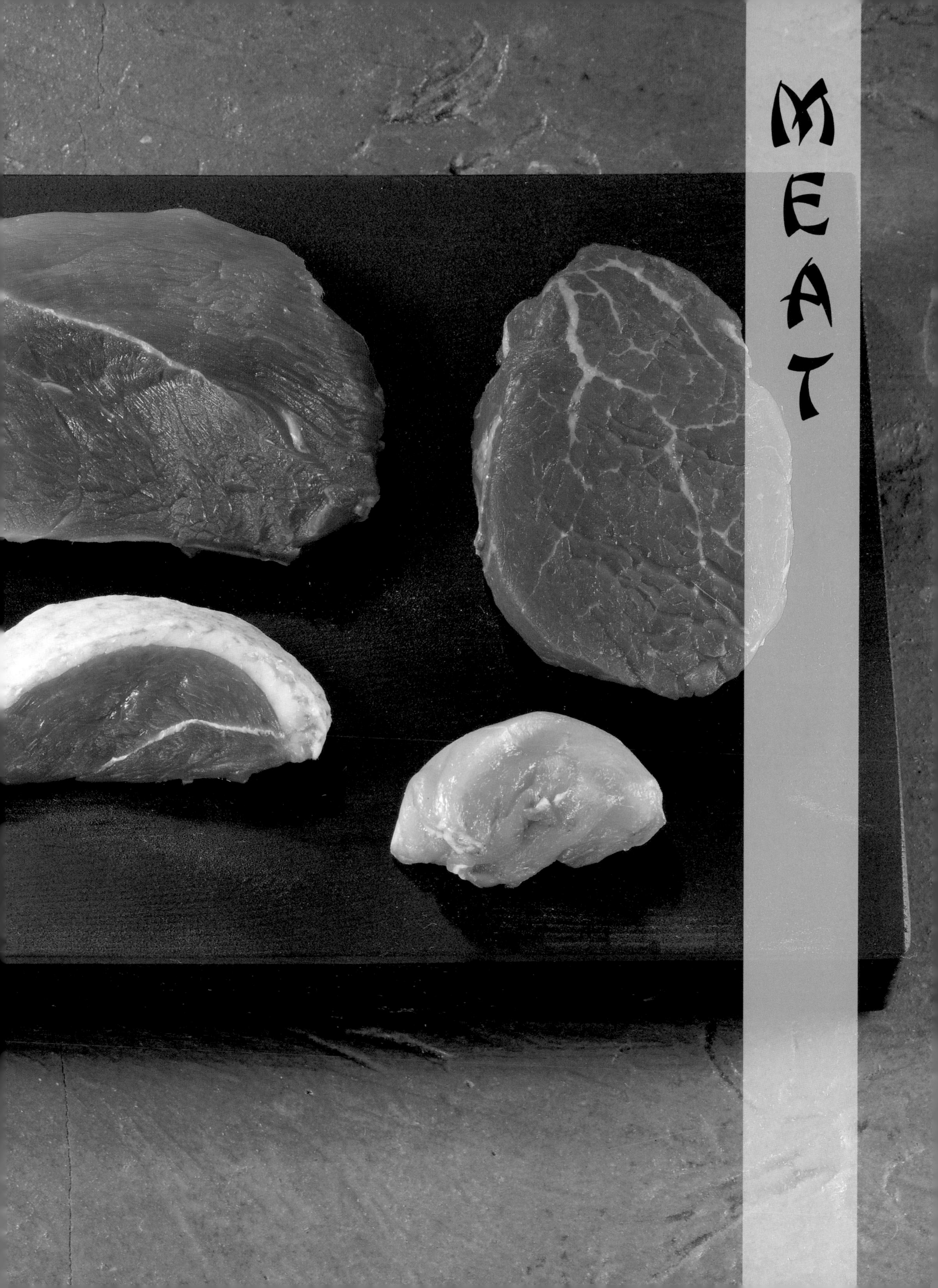

MEAT –
NOT A TRADITIONAL FOOD

Japan does not have an ancient tradition of meat-eating. As circumstances change, so a nation's eating habits change. The history of meat-eating in Japan has reflected the developments in Japanese society, in particular those that took place at the end of the last century.

In contrast to fish and seafood, which have always played an important rôle in Japanese cookery, meat only found its way into Japanese kitchens at the beginning of the nineteenth century.

Long before the time of the Buddhist ban on meat-eating, it had been quite common to eat meat, and certainly among the wealthier Japanese.

However, the eating of beef and horse-meat was never permitted. This was because these animals were generally used as beasts of burden and for transport. The ban on meat-eating was later born out of necessity. A great famine that affected the whole of Japan forced people to give up eating meat altogether and change to other foods. This famine affected the whole population.

Initially, the continued ban on meat-eating only concerned the Buddhist monks. But the rich, who were often to be seen in Buddhist monasteries and had frequent contacts with the monks, were quick to take up this 'fashion'. As a result, the ban soon spread across the country.

Although ordinary people were particularly badly hit by the famine, they wanted to maintain the same standards as the rich so they also adopted the ban on meat-eating. From then on, eating meat came to be seen as a sin.

This unwritten rule remained in force until the beginning of the nineteenth century. Then, quite suddenly, progressive Japanese people called for the ban to be lifted. They had developed very open attitudes towards the New World and were keen to try out anything that was different. so they were unwilling to do without beef any longer. They considered the strict ban to be long out of date and wanted to move with the times.

The ban was lifted following the opening of the Japanese borders to foreigners in 1873. An edict was issued by the emperor to the effect that henceforth meat-eating was to be allowed again. As soon as the borders opened recipes for meat dishes became available. These were tried out first in restaurants and later were introduced into the home.

Kobe Beef

This renaissance of meat-eating led to a very special Japanese practice, one that only involved beef. A Japanese would never consider eating a thick, fatty piece of pork, or what we might regard as a highly desirable cut of fillet steak with a fatty edge. Dishes containing fatty meat are still considered by the Japanese to be inedible. In Japan, the most highly-prized meat of all is kobe beef. This is a particular type of beef which has a white marbling of fat throughout the flesh. Since the Japanese like to eat their beef in paper-thin slices – in the form of sukiyaki and shabushabu or after it has been delicately marinated – the meat has to be prevented from drying out. Cattle that have simply been left to graze in the fields are not a reliable source of meat that has the desirable uniform marbling. Grazing cattle develop layers of fat only in certain parts of the body.

As a result, the Japanese had to develop an alternative to conventional livestock grazing methods. Japanese livestock spend the three short years of their lives receiving lavish attention. Although modern-day Japan has introduced cattle-sheds, animals receive the same care in the shed that they would in the pastures. Prize cattle spend their pampered lives on opulent farms. The water there is of the same excellent quality as the feed. The animals are given the kind of loving care normally only accorded to race-horses. They are massaged daily with either sake, beer or oil. The preferred substance, however, is gin. The result of all this daily massage is that the fat becomes evenly distributed over the animal's entire body. To ensure that the meat ends up with the desired fine, white fatty marbling, the masseur must practise his skills with great care and gentleness. In the last weeks of their lives, the cattle also receive a diet of beer in addition to the usual carefully selected feed. This seems to make them happy, but is actually only intended to fatten them up.

The finest meat of all is that with the most pronounced marbling. This meat, known as shimofuri, can command a very high price.

Kobe beef is a great luxury in Japan, as it has a very special flavour.

Do not despair if it proves impossible to find Kobe beef in our shops and supermarkets. For our purposes, ordinary beef is quite good enough as long as it has a good marbling of fat.

Pork and Poultry

Not so long ago, the Japanese quite simply regarded pork as inedible.

Nowadays, the eating of pork is no longer regarded with the same disdain. However, even today the Japanese will not eat just any cut of pork. A good fatty leg of pork will send a shiver down their spines, but they have no objection to lean, tender fillet of pork. Any cut of pork that still seems to be too fatty is made palatable by drowning it in copious quantities of green tea. In fact, green tea is mainly drunk in order to lose a little fat of one's own. A Japanese housewife would never stoop to using pork, however, in the case of dishes such as SUKIYAKI (page 104) or SHABUSHABU (page 101). For these, only the finest Kobe beef will do. Young and tender poultry, be it chicken, poussin or duck, is also very popular in Japanese cooking. Poultry is roasted, steamed, grilled and often minced and then used as a filling. A duck is even allowed to keep its fat, but only because the fat and skin can be roasted to a crispy texture.

BEEF ROULADE WITH SHALLOTS

Ingredients
200 g/7 oz beef,
preferably a slice of
steak 1½ cm/¾ in thick
1 shallot
3 tablespoons teriyaki
sauce (glazed soy sauce)

Method
Place the slice of beefsteak between layers of clingfilm and pound it with a steak hammer until its original thickness is reduced by half. Peel and quarter the shallot. Cut the slice of beef into four thin slices. Put one of the shallot quarters on each slice. Roll up the meat around the shallot and hold it in place with a small wooden skewer.
Preheat the grill. Using chopsticks, dip the rolls of meat into the teriyaki sauce and place them under the grill about 10 cm/4 in below the heat source, and cook until they are golden-brown. Dip the roulades into the sauce once again and grill them on the other side.

To serve
When they are ready, cut the roulades into 2 cm/1 in slices. With care, they can be cut so that the shallot is visible in the centre of the roulade. Arrange the slices neatly on a dish.

MARINATED SHOULDER OF PORK WITH NASTURTIUM FLOWERS

The Japanese cook their pork in green tea so as to eliminate some of the fatty taste.

Ingredients
1 pot of freshly brewed
green tea
800g/2 lb shoulder of
pork
300 ml/9 fl oz soy sauce
80 ml/2 fl oz sake
250 ml/8 fl oz cider
vinegar
3 tablespoons mirin
350 g/12 oz nasturtium
flowers
salt
2 tablespoons Japanese
mustard

Method
Bring the freshly-brewed tea to the boil in a saucepan and cook the meat gently in this for about 40 minutes. Then rinse the meat under the cold tap for a short time and leave to dry.

In a shallow bowl, combine the soy sauce, sake, cider vinegar and mirin. Leave the meat to stand, covered, in this marinade for two days, turning it occasionally. Wash the nasturtium flowers with care and blanch them briefly in boiling salted water. Leave them to drain and cool. Remove the meat from the marinade and cut into thin slices.

To serve
Arrange the meat on four plates and garnish with the flowers. The mustard and marinade should be divided up into four small bowls. Before the meat is eaten, it can be dipped into either the marinade or the mustard.

GRILLED FILLET OF BEEF WITH SOY SAUCE GLAZE

This dish, known as Teriyaki, can also be prepared on a hot stone. However, a charcoal or electric grill is equally suitable.

Method

Mix the mustard powder with a little hot water to make a thick paste and leave to stand for at least 15 minutes.

Pre-heat the electric or charcoal grill or the hot stone.

Warm the mirin in a saucepan over a medium heat. Remove the pan from the heat and flambé the mirin. Gently shake the pot from side to side until the flames are extinguished.

Stir the soy sauce and chicken stock into the mirin and bring this sauce briefly to the boil. As soon as it has boiled, remove the pot from the heat and allow the sauce to cool to room temperature.

When it has cooled, re-heat the sauce, adding the sugar. Meanwhile dissolve the cornflour in 1 tablespoon cold water. Just before the sauce reaches boiling point, reduce the heat and stir in the cornflour. Continue stirring until the sauce becomes clear and syrupy.

Stir the mustard into this glaze andreserve the mixture in a bowl.

Cut the beef into 12 5 mm/¼ inch slices.

First dip the slices into the glaze and then grill them for 1 minute on each side until they are golden-brown. If the meat is to be eaten 'well done', grill each piece for a further minute.

To serve

When the meat is ready, cut it into finger-sized slices and serve on four dinner plates. Pour a little extra glaze over each portion and garnish with parsley.

Ingredients

4 teaspoons mustard powder
250 ml/8 fl oz soy sauce
250 ml/8 fl oz mirin
250 ml/8 fl oz chicken stock
15 g/1 oz sugar
2 tablespoons cornflour
750 g/1½ lb lean fillet of beef or beef steak
small bunch parsley

FILLET OF BEEF COOKED ON A HOT STONE

There is no need to buy the 'grilling stone' sold in specialist cookware shops to prepare this recipe. A large flat stone of the kind that you can pick up on a river bank or on the beach will do perfectly well. Of course, it must be cleaned thoroughly before use.

Ingredients
600 g/1¼ lb fillet of beef
100 g/4 oz assorted mushrooms
4 abalone
20 mangetout peas
1 stick celery
1 stick leek
⅓ white radish (daikon or mooli)
small bunch chives
80 ml/3 fl oz soy sauce
80 ml/3 fl oz lemon juice
oregano
sesame seeds
oil

Method
Preheat the oven to its highest setting.
Cut the fillet of beef into medium-sized steaks. Wash the mushrooms and drain.
Remove the abalone from the shell. Clean them and then cut into 5 mm/¼ inch slices.
Wash the mangetout peas.
Wash the celery and leek and cut them both into 5 cm/2 in lengths.
Peel the radish and wash the chives and then slice them into tiny rings.
Now put the stone into the oven.
Combine the soy sauce with the lemon juice. Divide this sauce into two portions. Stir the radish and chives into one portion, and the oregano and sesame seeds into the other. Distribute the sauce among the four bowls.

To serve
Place all the ingredients on one serving dish.
Carefully remove the stone from the oven and put it on the table over a heatproof base. Brush a little oil on the stone. Cook the meat and then the other ingredients on the stone. Before eating them, dip them into the sauces. There is a ready-made sauce, available from Japanese food shops, which goes well with this dish. It is called yakinikunotare.

Fillet of Beef Cooked on a Hot Stone

MARINATED BEEF

Marinating the beef for two days makes the meat especially tender and gives it a wonderful aroma.

Ingredients
4 tablespoons sake
180 ml/6 fl oz rice vinegar
1 tablespoon sugar
90 ml/4 fl oz soy sauce
½ lemon
1 garlic clove
1 onion
konasansho
500 g/1 lb 2oz rump steak oil

Method
Bring the sake to the boil in a saucepan with the rice vinegar. As soon as it has boiled, add the sugar and soy sauce. Stir well to dissolve the sugar.
Cut the lemon half into two quarters and slice each of these very thinly. Peel the garlic and onion. Crush the garlic and chop the onion finely. Add the lemon, garlic, onion and konasansho to the sauce and reserve. Dice the meat into medium-sized cubes, season with salt and pepper and leave to stand for 30 minutes.
Cook the meat quickly in hot oil. The meat should not be allowed to cook through, the redness should just disappear from the surface.
Drain the meat on a kitchen towel. It should be thoroughly dry, so that it absorbs the sauce.

Put the sauce and the meat in a bowl and leave to marinate. Make sure the bowl is large enough for the sauce to cover all of the meat.
Cover the bowl with a plate and leave it in a cool place for two days.

To serve
Remove the meat from the sauce and cut it into very thin slices. Divide the meat between four plates and pour the sauce over each portion.

BEEF SLICES DIPPED IN STOCK

This dish, known in Japan as Shabushabu, is a favourite meat dish. Its name is derived from the sound that is heard when the slices of meat are drawn through the stock. To Japanese ears, this sounds like 'shabushabu'.

Method

Cut the frozen beef into wafer-thin slices and arrange it on a serving dish, taking care that the individual slices do not stick together.

Wash the celery and cut it into quarters.

Wash the carrots and the leeks. Cut each in half lengthways.

Peel the onions and cut into quarters.

Put the stewing meat and prepared vegetables in a casserole with 3 l/5¼ pints of water and simmer over a low heat for 4 hours. Skim the foam from the surface of the stock from time to time.

Strain the meat and stock through a sieve.

Leave the harusame to soak in cold water for 30 minutes and then cut into 10-cm/4-in lengths.

Wash the spring onions and cut into 5 cm/2 in lengths.

Wash the Chinese cabbage and cut into bite-sized squares.

To make the sesame sauce, mix the sesame paste, fish stock, 8 tablespoons of the soy sauce, the garlic clove and the rice vinegar, stirring well.

Make a ponzu sauce by stirring the remaining soy sauce into the lime juice.

Peel and grate the radish. Wash the chives and chop finely.

To serve

Arrange the prepared vegetables neatly on four plates. Divide the sauces between four bowls each.

Mix the sesame sauce, chopped chives and togarashi.

Season the ponzu sauce with the radish.

Fill a Mongolian hot pot (or a large casserole) three-quarters full with the clear stock and place it on a portable hot-plate at the table. Bring the liquid to the boil. Use chopsticks to alternate between dipping meat and vegetables first into the hot stock for a short time and then into the sauces.

Ingredients

800 g/2½ lb frozen tenderloin of beef
½ head of celery
2 carrots
2 leeks
3 onions
500 g/1lb 2oz lean stewing meat, on the bone
100 g/4 oz harusame (glass noodles)
4 spring onions
1 bunch Chinese leaves
500 g/1lb 2oz tofu
100 g/4 oz sesame paste
3 tablespoons fish stock
180 ml/6 fl oz soy sauce
2 teaspoons rice vinegar
juice of 1 lime
togarashi
1 white radish (daikon or mooli)
1 bunch chives
1 clove garlic, crushed

Overleaf:
Beef Slices Dipped in Stock

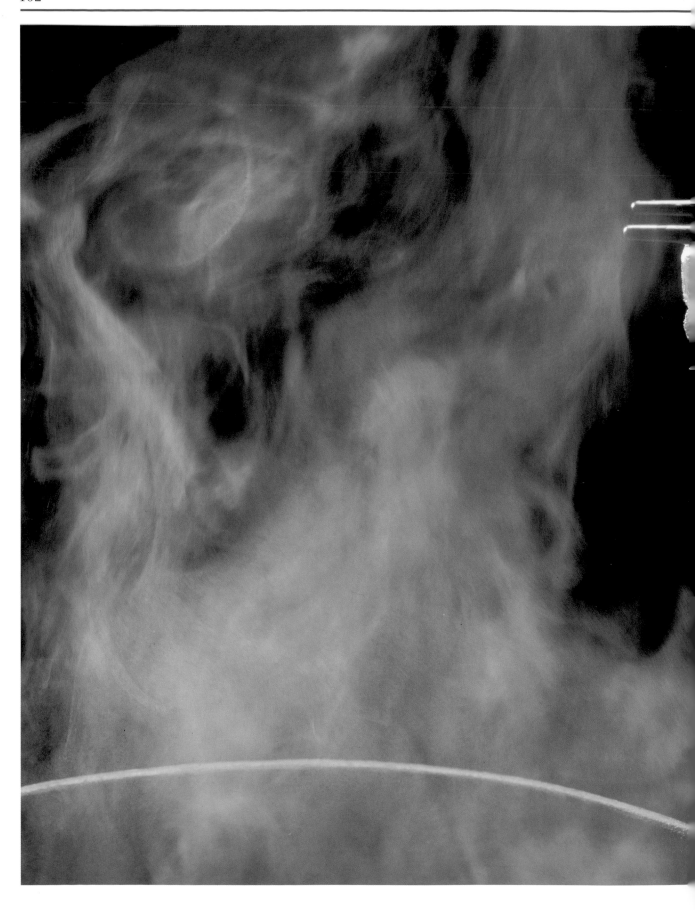

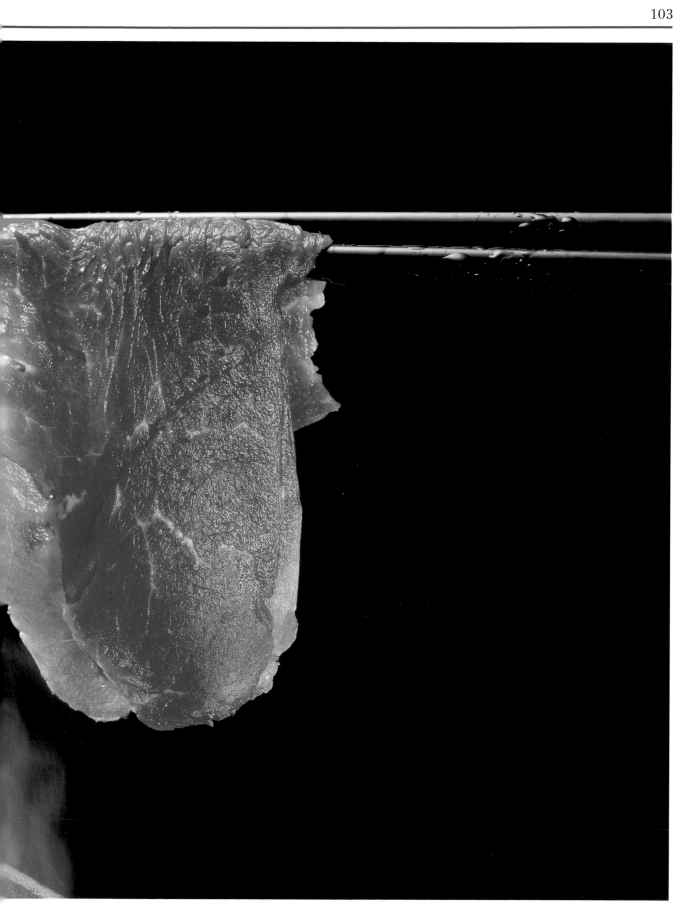

BEEF FONDUE

Along with tempura, beef fondue, called Sukiyaki in Japan, is one of the best-known Japanese dishes in the West. Fondue fans will welcome the chance to try something a little different.

Ingredients

400 g/14 oz frozen tenderloin or fillet of beef
100 g/4 oz harusame (glass noodles)
250 g/9 oz tofu
8 shiitake mushrooms
8 tender young spring onions
150 g/6 oz young Swiss chard leaves
3 tablespoons sake
3 tablespoons fish stock
3 tablespoons mirin
100 ml/4 fl oz soy sauce
3 tablespoons sugar
1 tablespoon oil

Method

Cut the frozen beef first into wafer-thin slices and then into seven centimetre/three inch lengths.

Cook the harusame in boiling water for about five minutes.

Dice the tofu into 2- cm/1- in cubes and drain.

Wash the shiitake mushrooms. Discard the stems and make two cuts in the caps in the shape of a cross.

Wash the spring onions and cut them diagonally into 5 cm /2 in lengths. Remove the tough stalks of the Swiss chard and cut the leaves into halves or quarters depending on their size.

Warm the sake, mirin, soy sauce, fish stock and sugar in a saucepan until the sugar has dissolved.

To serve

Heat the oil in a fondue pan on the cooker ring and fry 5 or 6 slices of beef.

When they look to be half-cooked, add half of the prepared stock and a third of all the other ingredients to the pan.

As soon as the vegetables are cooked, transfer the pan to the dinner table and leave the sukiyaki to cook on a portable hot-plate.

The fondue meal is now ready.

The diners use chopsticks to put small portions of the fondue into their individual bowls.

The remaining meat and vegetables are gradually added to the pot and cooked during the course of the meal.

If the stock has reduced too far, the liquid can simply be topped up with cold water or dashi (for recipe, see page 152).

CHICKEN KEBABS

Meat balls made from three varieties of minced meat as well as chicken breast and chicken liver are cooked together on skewers.

Method

Bring the mirin, sugar and soy sauce to the boil in a saucepan. Stir well until the sauce reduces to a syrupy consistency. Pour it into a sauceboat and leave to cool.

Combined the different minced meats. Peel and the onion and garlic; crush the garlic and grate the onion. Mix the onion and garlic into the minced meats and shape the mixture into meatballs 2 cm/1 in in diameter. Dice the chicken breast into 2-3 cm/1 in cubes and halve the chicken liver. Cut the white parts of the leeks into 5 cm/2 in lengths.

Soak the bamboo skewers in water for 30 minutes, then thread them with a meatball, a piece of chicken breast, a piece of leek and a chicken liver, in that order. Do not bunch the ingredients too tightly together on the skewers as they need space to grill evenly.

Heat a little oil in a grill-pan. Sprinkle a little lemon juice over each skewer and then baste each one with the sauce. Grill the skewers, turning and basting them frequently. Keep turning the skewers and brush on a little more sauce if necessary. Clean the pan after each grilling session, as the sauce can caramelise and burn.

To serve

Serve the skewers on a serving-dish, add a few drops of lemon juice and a sprinkle of shichimi togarashi.

Ingredients

125 ml/4 fl oz soy sauce
3 tablespoons mirin
3 tablespoons sugar
100 g/4 oz lean minced beef
100 g/4 oz lean minced pork
100 g/4 oz minced chicken
1 onion
1 garlic clove
400 g/14 oz chicken breast fillets with skin
200 g/7 oz chicken livers
2 leeks
oil
2 teaspoons lemon juice
shichimi togarashi

CHICKEN FILLET WITH SHISO LEAVES

Method

Stir 1 tablespoon of sake into the miso with the sugar and 1 tablespoon of mirin. Leave the fillet in this marinade for at least 12 hours, preferably overnight. The next day, remove the meat from the marinade, drain and then cut into 6 equal portions. Wrap a shiso leaf around each portion. Mix the soy sauce with the remaining sake and mirin.

Pre-heat the grill to its highest setting. Grill the wrapped pieces of chicken breast fillet all over until they are well browned.

To serve

Arrange the meat on the plates. Place a small bowl of the sauce at each place setting. The diners dip the meat in the sauce before eating it.

Ingredients:

180 g/6 fl oz dark miso (akamiso)
3 tablespoons sake
2 tablespoons sugar
2½ tablespoons mirin
200 g/7 oz chicken breast fillets
6 shiso leaves
1 tablespoon soy sauce

FILLET OF POUSSIN WITH SESAME SAUCE

Radicchio or red-leaved chicory is a popular Italian vegetable which is becoming more easily found in Britain.

Ingredients
400 g/14 oz poussin breast fillets
1 large sweet orange
60 g/3 oz radicchio
8 chives
90 g/4 oz white sesame seeds
4 teaspoons sugar
2½ tablespoons soy sauce
4 tablespoons fish stock

Method
Cook the poussin breast in lightly-salted water for about 20 minutes. Leave the meat to cool in its stock. Meanwhile, peel the orange carefully so that none of the pith adheres to the fruit. Split it into segments and remove the skin from each segment.
Wash the radicchio and remove the leaves. Cut the larger leaves up into two or three pieces. Wash the chives and chop them into short strips. Drain the meat and slice it thinly.
Toast the white sesame seeds in a dry frying-pan until you can smell their aroma. Pound half the sesame seeds in a mortar and add these and the rest of the seeds to the fish stock with the sugar and soy sauce.

Pour a little sauce over the poussin and leave it to stand for 10 minutes. Arrange the radicchio and orange segments on four shallow bowls. Add the poussin and pour the sesame sauce over it. Leave to stand for a further 10 minutes before serving.

To serve
Garnish each plate with a few chopped chives.

CHICKEN WITH RADISH AND WINE

Ingredients
400 g/14 oz raw chicken fillet, skinned
200 g/7 oz white radish (daikon or mooli)
300 ml/9 fl oz water
1 teaspoon sugar
2-3 tablespoons soy sauce
2 tablespoons mirin
3-4 tablespoons dry red wine

Method
Wash and dry the meat. Cut it into 3 cm/1 in cubes.
Peel the radish and cut into 2.5 cm/1 in cubes. Boil the water with the sugar and soy sauce. Add the meat and radish and simmer gently for about 15 minutes over a low heat. Add the mirin to the stock and cook the meat for a further 5 to 10 minutes. Add the red wine and continue cooking for another 2 minutes.

To serve
Pour the mixture into soup bowls.

Fillet of Poussin with Sesame Sauce

MARINATED, DEEP-FRIED POUSSIN

Ginger juice is the liquid from red pickled ginger roots.

Ingredients
*400 g/14 oz poussin
breast fillets
3 tablespoons soy sauce
2 tablespoons sake
cornflour
1 teaspoon ginger juice
12 small sweet red
peppers
oil for deep-frying*

Method
Cut the poussin breast fillets into 3 cm/1 in cubes.
To make the marinade, combine the soy sauce, sake, cornflour and ginger juice. Marinate the cubes of meat for about 1 hour, turning frequently.
Clean the peppers and discard the seeds, then cut them into strips. Take the meat out of the marinade and leave to drain.

Heat the oil until a 2.5 cm/1 in cube of bread will brown in 60 seconds. First, quickly deep-fry the peppers. Remove them, drain them on kitchen paper, and replace them with the cubes of chicken. Fry the chicken until it is golden-brown all over. Drain it on kitchen paper.

To serve
Combine the peppers and the chicken. Serve them on four plates.

MIXED SALAD WITH HOT MEAT SAUCE

Ingredients
*generous pinch dried
wakame
4 savoy cabbage leaves
10 cm/4 in snake gourd
small bunch chives
100 g/4 oz soya bean
sprouts
100 g/4 oz tinned
bamboo shoots
1 garlic clove
1 slice fresh ginger
1 onion
1½ tablespoons oil
150 g/6 oz minced pork
3 tablespoons sake
100 g/4 oz dark miso
(akamiso)
pepper
1 tablespoon sesame oil*

Method
Leave the wakame to soak in water for 10 minutes, then dip it briefly in boiling water before leaving it to drain. Clean all the vegetables and cut them into pieces the size of matchsticks. Chop the bamboo shoots and wakame in the same way, leaving them both to drain.
Peel and chop the garlic, ginger and onion into thin slices. Then fry all three together in hot oil until their aromas are released.
Add the pork and fry until golden-brown. Pour the sake over the mixture in the pan. Combine the miso with 250 ml/8 fl oz water and add it to the pan. Mix well and continue cooking until all the liquid has evaporated. Season with a generous sprinkling of pepper and a few drops of sesame oil.

To serve
Divide the salad between four bowls and pour the meat sauce over the salad.

DEEP-FRIED AUBERGINES STUFFED WITH MINCED MEAT

Although aubergines are a mild-flavoured vegetable, this dish is quite hot and spicy because of the white radish and chilies. Ginger juice is the liquid from red pickled ginger roots.

Method

Combine the meat with the egg yolk, cornflour, 3 tablespoons of the soy sauce and the ginger juice. Wash the aubergine and cut it in half lengthways. Then cut it into slices 3 mm/⅛ in thick. Sprinkle these with salt, leave to stand for a short time and pat them dry with a clean tea towel. Then toss them in flour.

Place some of the meat filling on a slice of aubergine. Place a second slice on top of this and hold it in place with a cocktail stick. Use all the aubergine and the meat mixture in this way.

In a saucepan, heat up the stock with the rest of the soy sauce and the mirin to make a sauce. Reserve the sauce.

Cut the noodles into 5 cm/2 in lengths with a pair of scissors.

Cut the nori leaf into eight strips of equal size and use them to tie the glass noodles into eight little bundles..

Wash the red chili peppers.

Heat the oil until a 2.5 cm/1 in cube of bread will brown in 60 seconds. Deep-fry the filled aubergines, red peppers and bundles of noodles.

To serve

Arrange the deep-fried foods on four plates.

Add small portions of white radish, spring onions and ginger to eat plate.

Pour the sauce into four small bowls.

The diners dip the aubergine slices, red peppers and noodles into the sauce and then sprinkle the slices with the radish, grated ginger and spring onions.

Ingredients

100 g/4 oz minced beef
100 g/4 oz minced pork
1 egg yolk
1 tablespoon cornflour
4 tablespoons soy sauce
1 teaspoon ginger juice
1 aubergine
salt
flour
240 ml/8 fl oz stock
4 tablespoons mirin
½ nori leaf
100 g/4 oz soaked harusame (glass noodles)
12 red chili peppers
oil for deep-frying
6 tablespoons grated white radish (daikon or mooli)
4 tablespoons chopped spring onions
2 tablespoons grated ginger

CHICKEN MEATBALLS WITH NASTURTIUM FLOWERS

Like so many Japanese dishes, this is a feast for the eyes and a treat for the taste-buds.

Ingredients

400 g/14 oz tofu
400 g/14 oz minced chicken
15 mangetout peas
8 shiitake mushrooms
1 small carrot
8 shiso leaves
1 egg
salt
3 tablespoons mirin
3 tablespoons soy sauce
3 teaspoons sugar
oil for deep-frying
200 g/7 oz nasturtium flowers
1 leek
600 ml/1 pint meat stock
2 teaspoon ground ginger

Method

Wrap the tofu in a tea towel and leave a weight on it for 2 hours, so that it loses some of its liquid and becomes firmer. Then add the tofu to the minced chicken and purée them in a blender.

Wash and chop finely the mangetout peas, mushrooms, carrot and shiso leaves. Add all these to the purée.

Beat the egg with a little salt, the mirin, 1 tablespoon of the soy sauce and two teaspoons of the sugar. Then add to the mixture and stir in well.

Heat the oil in a deep-fryer until a 2.5 cm/1 in cube of bread will brown in 60 seconds. Shape the mixture into meatballs about 3 cm/1 in. in diameter. Deep-fry in the hot oil until they are golden brown.

Leave the meat balls to drain well on paper towels.

Blanch the nasturtium flowers in boiling water for 2 minutes and drain them.

Wash the leek and cut it into very thin strips.

Bring the meat stock to the boil. Add the meat balls and cover the saucepan. Reduce the heat and cook for 5 minutes.

Then stir in the remaining mirin and sugar and allow it all to stand for a further 5 minutes. Add the remaining soy sauce, stir well and cook on a high heat for 5 minutes more. Remove the pan from the heat and leave the meat balls and stock to cool.

To serve

Remove the meat balls from the saucepan with a slotted spoon and put them into four small bowls. Pour some of the stock over each portion and garnish with the strips of leek and the nasturtium flowers.

Finally, sprinkle a little ground ginger over each portion.

GRILLED CHICKEN BREASTS

Method

Cut the chicken breast into four pieces of about the same size. Cut the lime into wafer-thin slices. Wash the cress. Mix the soy sauce, mirin and sake in a shallow baking dish and add four slices of lime. Place the fillet in this marinade for 30 minutes.

Pre-heat the grill. Remove the meat from the marinade and grill until it is golden-brown. Baste with the marinade and grill again until the meat turns a deeper brown. Then cut it into bite-sized chunks.

To serve

Arrange the fillets of poussin and the cress on four plates and garnish with the slices of lime.

Ingredients

2 × 200 g/7 oz boned chicken breast
1 untreated lime
1 punnet of cress
6 tablespoons soy sauce
6 tablespoons mirin
3 tablespoons sake

CHICKEN ON A BED OF VEGETABLES

Method

Steep the mushrooms in lukewarm water for 20 minutes. Then remove their stems, reserve the liquid and add water to make it up to at least 500 ml/16 fl oz.

Peel the carrots and salsify. Wash the leeks and allow the lotus roots to drain. Cut the carrots, salsify and leeks into 2 cm/1 in lengths, reserving a few pieces of leek. Cut the lotus root into thin slices and sprinkle it with a few drops of vinegar. Cut the chicken meat into 2.5 cm/1 in cubes and sprinkle with salt.

Heat 1 tablespoon of oil in a frying-pan and fry the chunks of chicken until they are golden-brown. Add the remaining oil and all the vegetables, and fry for just 1 minute. Add the mushroom liquid and the sugar and cook covered for 5 minutes over a medium heat. Remove the lid, add the soy sauce and mirin and cook for a further 20 minutes, or until the liquid has reduced by half.

To serve

Serve in a large bowl and sprinkle the reserved pieces of chopped leek over the mixture.

Ingredients

4 dried shiitake mushrooms
100 g/4 oz carrots
100 g/4 oz salsify
100 g/4 oz leeks
100 g/4 oz tinned lotus roots
1 tablespoon wine or rice vinegar
300 g/11 oz filleted chicken
salt
2 tablespoons oil
1 tablespoon sugar
4 tablespoons soy sauce
2 tablespoons mirin

TOFU

TOFU WITH MANGETOUT

To the Japanese, the presentation of food, with the emphasis on harmony of colour and ingredients, is vitally important.

Ingredients
600 g/2½ lb tofu
12 mangetout peas
1 lime
500 ml/10 fl oz fish stock
20 × 20 cm/8 in kombu
4 tablespoons mirin
3 tablespoons sake
⅓ teaspoon salt
3 tablespoons light soy sauce
1 tablespoon chopped chives

Method
Wash the tofu pieces and wrap them in muslin or cheesecloth and freeze them overnight. The next day, wash and clean the mangetout peas. Peel the skin of the lime into wafer-thin strips and cut these into matchsticks.

Bring the kombu and the fish stock to the boil in a large pan. Remove the frozen tofu from the muslin and add it to the stock. Cook for 5 minutes, then add the sake, mirin, salt and soy sauce. Cook for 10 minutes over a low heat. Blanch the mangetout in 250 ml/8 fl oz of the stock. Plunge the mangetout into iced water immediately afterwards, so that they retain their bright green colour.

To serve
Cut each block of tofu into 8 pieces and divide these up among four small bowls. Garnish with the mangetout peas. Sprinkle with the slivers of lime peel and make an attractive arrangement with the slices of the lime.
A few strips of dried gourd, perhaps dipped in water and food colouring, can be used to tie up the tofu cubes, like sandwiches, with the mangetout peas as the sandwich filler.

Tofu with Mangetout

DEEP-FRIED TOFU STUFFED WITH MEAT

Ingredients
*2 dried shiitake
mushrooms
400 g/14 oz or 4 pieces
deep-fried tofu (atsuage)
100 g/4 oz minced beef
1 egg yolk
20 g/1 oz powdered
ginger
4 tablespoons sugar
1 teaspoon sake
pinch of salt
5 tablespoons soy sauce
500 ml/10 fl oz fish
stock
2 tablespoons mirin*

Method
Wash the shiitake mushrooms and soak in water for 20 minutes. Pour the soaking water off (reserve it for another dish) and chop the mushrooms finely.
Place the deep-fried tofu in a sieve and pour hot water over it. Combine the minced beef with the mushrooms, egg yolk, ginger, a little sugar, the sake, salt and ½ teaspoon of soy sauce. Make a slit in the side of each piece of tofu to form a pouch, fill this with the meat mixture and close the opening with a cocktail stick.

Bring the fish stock to the boil in a saucepan with the mirin, and the rest of the sugar and soy sauce. Once the stock has come to the boil, add the pieces of stuffed tofu and cook, covered, over a medium heat for about 20 minutes.

To serve
Cut the stuffed tofu slices in half diagonally and serve them in four small bowls with the sauce.

TOFU WITH AUBERGINES AND PAPRIKA

Ingredients
*300 g/11 oz tofu
oil
2 aubergines
2 sweet red peppers
2 tablespoons sesame
oil
4 tablespoons dark miso
4 tablespoons sugar
sansho powder*

Method
Press the tofu between two sheets of kitchen paper to firm it and pat it dry. Cut it into bite-sized pieces and fry in the hot oil until it is golden-brown on all sides.
Wash the aubergines and sweet peppers. Peel them and seed the peppers. Cut the aubergines and peppers into bite-sized pieces. Heat the sesame oil in a frying-pan and fry them on high heat.
Add the miso, sugar and 1 tablespoon water to the pan. Cook for another 2 minutes, the vegetables should be cooked but still crisp.

To serve
Leave the vegetables to cool and serve them with the tofu in four small bowls. Add a sprinkle of sansho powder to taste.

HOT TOFU

This dish is best prepared at the table. Hot tofu is at its most delicious when the pieces have just been warmed through in the stock.

Method

Wash the spring onions, dry them thoroughly and cut them into thin rings.

Toast the nori leaf on one side in a dry frying-pan and crumble the leaf into tiny pieces.

Toast the sesame seeds and pound them coarsely.

Peel the ginger and grate it finely.

Bring the fish stock, soy sauce, sake and mirin to the boil quickly.

As soon as the stock has boiled, stir in the katsuobushi, remove the saucepan from the heat and strain immediately.

Half fill a saucepan with water and add the kombu. Heat the water and kombu over a moderate heat.

Meanwhile cut the tofu into 3-cm/1 in cubes and add it to the hot, but not boiling, stock.

To serve

Heat up the sauce once again and pour it into small bowls.

Now remove the cubes of tofu from the hot stock, one piece at a time. Each piece is then dipped in a little sauce. Present the rings of spring onion, crumbled nori leaf, sesame and ginger as separate side-dishes.

Ingredients

2 spring onions
1 nori leaf
2 tablespoons sesame seeds
1 piece fresh ginger
240 ml/8 fl oz fish stock
120 ml/4 fl oz soy sauce
2 tablespoons sake
2 tablespoons mirin
1 tablespoon katsuobushi
5 × 5 cm/2 in kombu
600g/1¼ lb tofu

Overleaf:
Hot Tofu

VEGETABLE STEW WITH TOFU

Ingredients
*8 dried shiitake
mushrooms
dried gourd strips
500 g/1 lb 2 oz tofu
oil
1 small spring cabbage
100 g/4 oz mangetout
peas
1 bunch chives
4 eggs
2 tablespoons sugar
salt
2 tablespoons cornflour
80 g/3 oz (glass noodles)
1 nori leaf
20 × 20 cm/8 in kombu
1.5l/2½ pints fish stock
4 tablespoons soy sauce*

Method
Soak the mushrooms in plenty of water for 10 minutes. Add the strips of dried gourd.

Divide the tofu into rectangles 2 cm/1 in by 3 cm/1½ in and fry them in hot oil until golden-brown on all sides.

Wash the spring cabbage and the mangetout peas. Remove the hard stems of the cabbage and then blanch the leaves for a short time in boiling water.

Drain the mushrooms and strips of gourd, reserving the water. Finely chop the mushrooms and put some on each cabbage leaf and roll up the leaf. Use the gourd strips to tie the roll securely.

Wash the chives and tie them small bunches.

Beat the eggs, sugar, salt and cornflour. Heat a little oil in an omelette pan and make very thin pancakes with this batter. Roll up the pancakes and cut them into slices 5 cm/2 in wide.

Cook the noodles for 5 minutes in plenty of boiling water. Cut the nori leaf into 2 cm/1 in strips.

Cut the noodles into 10 cm/4 in lengths. Use the strips of nori leaf to tie small bundles of noodles together.

Cut the kombu into 5 cm/2 in wide strips.

Bring the fish stock to the boil and add the water that was used to soak the mushrooms and gourd.

Add all the ingredients to the stock except for the nori-wrapped noodles. Stick small bamboo skewers into the ingredients. Once the stew has come to the boil, remove the kombu and then place the stew on a portable hotplate so that it stays warm.

To serve
Bring the stew to the table and keep it warm on a hot-plate.

The diners use bamboo skewers to skewer the ingredients and put them on their own plates or bowls.

When the vegetables and tofu have been eaten, the stock can be poured out into bowls.

Vegetable Stew with Tofu

SURPRISE PACKETS

A surprise packet is like the future – you can never be sure of what it will hold.

Ingredients
4 dried oyster mushrooms
4 thin slices of deep-fried tofu
8 quails' eggs
100g/4 oz fillet of chicken breast, skinned and boned
8 gingko nuts
300 ml/10 fl oz fish stock
4 teaspoons soy sauce
2 tablespoons sake
2 teaspoons sugar

Method
Place the mushrooms in a bowl in plenty of warm water. Soak them for at least 1 hour.
Cut the slices of tofu in half lengthways and carefully cut a slit in each piece to form a pouch.
Bring plenty of water to the boil in a large pan and cook the slices of deep-fried tofu for about 2 minutes. Use the same water to boil the quails' eggs for 3 minutes. Cut the meat into 1 cm/ cubes. Then take the mushrooms out of their water and cut them into very thin strips.

Mix all the prepared ingredients together and use this mixture to fill the pouches in the tofu pieces. Place the stuffed tofu slices in a large pan and add the fish stock. Season with the soy sauce, sake and sugar. Cook the surprise packets for 15 minutes over a medium heat. Then reduce the heat to its lowest setting and leave the parcels to stand in the stock for at least another 2 hours.

To serve
Arrange the surprise packets on four small plates.

SPICY TOFU

Ingredients
600g/2¼ lb tofu
2 spring onions
1 piece ginger root
4 shiso leaves
1 tablespoon oil
2 tablespoons soy sauce
1 tablespoon mirin
1 teaspoon sake

Method
Drain the tofu well. Cut it into 5 131
cm/2 in cubes and put them in a bowl.
Wash the spring onions and chop them very finely. Peel the ginger and grate well. Cut the shiso leaves into thin strips.
Heat the oil in a frying-pan and fry half of the ginger for a short time. Then add the soy sauce, mirin and sake. Mix well and allow the mixture to come to the boil for a few seconds. Leave to cool.

Once the sauce has cooled to room temperature, pour it over the tofu and leave the mixture to stand, covered, for one hour.

To serve
Divide the spicy tofu up among four small bowls and garnish with the remaining spring onions and shiso leaves.

SWEET AND SOUR TOFU

Method

Cut the tofu into 2.5 cm/1 in cubes. Prepare a marinade using half the soy sauce and a little shichimi. Marinate the cubes of tofu for 10 minutes.
Wash the spring onions and cut them into thin rings.
Peel the carrots and cut into julienne strips.
Cut the bamboo shoots into wafer-thin slices.

Blanch the spring onions and carrots in a little boiling water for 2 minutes.
Meanwhile bring the rest of the soy sauce to the boil, adding the rice vinegar, mirin, sake and sugar and keep the sauce boiling until all the sugar has dissolved.

To serve

Remove the tofu cubes from the marinade. Divide them among four small bowls and add the vegetables to each bowl.
Finally, pour the hot sauce over the mixture and sprinkle with a little shichimi togarashi.

Ingredients

400 g/14 oz tofu
100 ml/4 fl oz soy sauce
shichimi togarashi
small bunch spring onions
150 g/6 oz carrots
150 g/6 oz canned bamboo shoots
4 tablespoons rice vinegar
2 tablespoons mirin
2 tablespoons sake
3 tablespoons sugar

FRIED TOFU WITH SESAME

Method

Cut the tofu 12 pieces and dust each piece with flour.
Peel the radish and the ginger and grate both finely. Wash the chives and cut into short lengths.

Heat about 500 ml/16 fl oz sesame oil in a deep fryer and fry the tofu pieces over a medium heat until golden brown all over. While they are frying, toast the sesame seeds in a dry frying-pan, until they give off a pleasant aroma.
Add the toasted sesame seeds, ginger and radish to the tofu and allow the mixture to stand for 10 minutes.

To serve

Divide the tofu and sesame mixture among four small bowls and pour the soy sauce over it.
Sprinkle the chopped chives over each bowl.

Ingredients

600g/2¼ lb tofu
flour
⅓ white radish (daikon or mooli)
1 piece fresh ginger
1 bunch chives
sesame oil for frying
6 tablespoons sesame seeds
1 tablespoon soy sauce

SWEETS

TEMPTING LITTLE DELICACIES

In Japan, eating sweets is by no means the exclusive preserve of children. Adults are only too happy to indulge in a sweetmeat or two. A ladies' tea party, for example, would be quite unthinkable without a selection of sweetmeats.

As is the case with dishes prepared from vegetables, fish or meat, the selection and presentation of sweets should be in harmony with the time of day and the season.

In modern-day Japan, there are a still a few old family firms that specialise in making sweets and confectionery in the traditional style. Confectionery should appeal to all the senses. The flavour must not be too pronounced, otherwise it might spoil the delicate aroma of the tea. It should look attractive, and at the same time its colour and shape should say something about its flavour.

These criteria hold good for every occasion. They are just as important for a simple gift at a children's party as for a wedding present, a sweetmeat for a ladies' tea party or an elegantly wrapped gift for your host.

The basic ingredients in Japanese confectionery are few and simple. It is therefore all the more astonishing that such a remarkable variety of little treats can be made from them. For example, a skilled confectioner will fashion sweetened bean paste into a perfect replica of a maple leaf. From one day or one month to the next, the shape and colour of the leaves will be varied to reflect the actual changes on leaves on a tree outside the window. In spring, another confectioner might prepare a sweetmeat which is a perfect representation of a cherry blossom. In summer, one might be fashioned to resemble the small, golden leaves of a blossom. The autumn is the time to produce confectionery in the shape of mushrooms and pine needles, while in winter, little white tablets will be on offer showing the 'imprint' of tiny animal paws.

In the course of a typical Japanese afternoon, friends may be found sitting together on a small terrace, drinking tea, chatting or simply admiring the view.

Is that Mount Fuji they can see up there, just behind the clouds? Fuji is the very symbol of all that is sovereign, great and beautiful, but it is also an image of ever-present danger. For it is, of course, an active volcano – and, as such, it has a mystical hold over the people.

At least once in every Japanese person's life, he or she is expected to climb Mount Fuji. Even the smallest and remotest villages send one of their number up this holy mountain. They all brave it to the top, for it is here that the temple stands. Let us leave the friends gathered at tea to venerate the mountain. One or other of them may already have been to the top, others have yet to make the journey. There it stands, in the far distance and yet also on the plate just in front of them. Fuji – just one of many varieties of confectionery.

FRUIT AND CONFECTIONERY INGREDIENTS

Bean paste: A dark-red, sweet paste made from kidney beans. It is used in a wide variety of sweets in Japan.

Chestnuts: In our recipes these are used peeled, boiled and soaked in syrup.

Confectionery: Sweets made from bean paste, agar-agar, and rice flour, all skilfully shaped and coloured.

Kaki: This is the persimmon, also known as Sharon fruit. It is native to China, but has been grown in Japan for centuries. It is also grown in the United States and the Middle East and is available in Europe in late autumn and winter. The kaki looks like an orange tomato. When soft, the it has a delicious flavour, a little like a very sweet, fresh apricot. Dried kaki, known as *Hoshikaki,* are served as a sweet to accompany tea, especially at New Year.

Kiwi fruit: Also known as Chinese gooseberries, these are an oval-shaped fruit, weighing about 60-100 g/2-3 oz, with a hard, rust-coloured, slightly furry skin. The flesh of the fruit is a bright, trans-lucent green, dotted with tiny black seeds. Kiwis impart a bitter taste to all dishes containing dairy products as they contain actinidin, an enzyme which digests protein. The effect of the enzyme can be neutralised if the fruit is immersed in hot water.

Kumquats: These tiny fruits look like miniature oranges, but unlike oranges, the skin of kumquats can be eaten along with the fruit. Kumquats have a spicy sweet-and-sour orange flavour. They come in two varieties, nagami, which are oval and meiwa which are rounded and slightly larger.

Mochi rice: Mochi or glutinous rice, the type of rice always used in desserts. Unlike uruchi rice, it is cooked in a steamer, tipped into a wooden container and beaten into a glutinous consistency. Mochi rice can be used in a cake filling. It is also sold in powdered form as *Joshinko.*

Nashi: The Japanese or Asian pear, which has a smooth, russet skin and firm, juicy, opalescent flesh with a subtle but obvious taste of pear. The shape and consistency are, however, closer to that of an apple. It is eaten raw and tastes sweeter if peeled first.

Soya milk: Milk made from soya bean paste and boiled with fresh water.

Strawberry: These red fruits are also very popular in Japan.

Sweet Potato: Despite the name, sweet potatoes are not actually related to the potato. They are rounded, long or spindly with a pointed end. The skin colour varies from white to golden- brown or reddish-pink. The flesh is sweet and is either whitish or yellow. Sweet potatoes taste best when roasted in hot ashes.

Yokan: A sweet bean paste. Red bean paste (kuroan, see page 155) is mixed with seaweed or wheat flour and shaped into rolls about 5 cm/2 in long. Yokan is served with tea in 2 cm/1 in slices.

Yuzu: The Japanese lime is the size of a mandarin orange and has a yellowish skin. The flesh is extremely tart and inedible. The skin is used to season salads or add a spicy fragrance to sweets, and the juice can be used to enhance sauces.

GREEN TEA JELLY

This simple but very clever little snack is sometimes an acquired taste for European palates.

Ingredients
8g/¼ oz agar-agar
5g/¼ oz powdered green tea
150 g/6 oz sugar
3 tablespoons mirin
6 kumquats

Method
Leave the agar-agar to soak in 250 ml/8 fl oz of warm water.

Once the agar-agar has dissolved, add the tea to the liquid and beat the mixture with a whisk. Add the sugar and mirin and let it all come briefly to the boil before removing it from the heat.
Pour the jelly into a hexagonal bowl with tall sides and leave it to cool and set.

To serve
Once it has set, cut the jelly into cubes or thin slices and serve garnished with the kumquats.

PANCAKES

The markings made on the surface of these sweet pancakes should resemble fish.

Ingredients
90 g/4 oz flour
½ teaspoon baking powder
1 egg
75 g/3 oz sugar
½ teaspoon mirin
120 g/5 oz sweetened red bean paste
1 tablespoon oil

Method
Sift the flour with the baking powder. Whisk the egg white in a bowl until stiff. Then add the sugar and beat together until the mixture forms stiff peaks.
Combine the egg yolk, mirin and 2 tablespoons water and stir carefully. Finally fold in the flour.

Heat 1 tablespoon oil in an omelette or frying-pan. Slowly pour in the batter. As soon as the batter starts to set, use a wooden spoon or spatula to coax it into an oval shape. Cover the pan and cook the pancake over a medium heat.

When it is ready, slide the pancake carefully from the pan. Spread the bean paste on the surface and fold it over once.

To serve
Heat a metal skewer and use it to draw the outline of a fish on the pancake.

SWEET POTATOES IN THEIR JACKETS

This is a really exquisite dessert that would grace any table.

Method

Pre-heat the oven to 175°C/375°F/Gas Mark 3.

Wash the sweet potatoes thoroughly, but do not peel them. Bake them in the oven for about 70 minutes.

When they are ready, cut the potatoes in half lengthways and hollow them out almost down to their skins.

Set aside the hollowed out skins and purée the potato flesh.

Cook the puréed potatoes with the butter, the sugar and the whipping cream in a pan over a medium heat until they thicken slightly. Stir frequently with a wooden spoon.

Remove the saucepan from the heat, stir in 1 egg yolk and reheat the mixture.

Remove the saucepan from the heat once again and stir in the brandy. Put this potato mixture back into the hollowed-out potato skins, heaping it generously; smooth the surface.

Mix the second egg yolk with the mirin and brush a generous coating over the potato mixture.

Bake the potatoes once more in the oven until they are golden-brown, about 15 minutes.

To serve

Place the golden-brown halves of sweet potato on a plate. Serve them while they are still warm.

Ingredients

200 g/7 oz sweet potatoes
40 g/1½ oz butter
70 g/3 oz sugar
250 ml/8 fl oz whipping cream
4 teaspoons brandy
2 egg yolks
1 tablespoon mirin

TEA

undisturbed, reminding guests of the gentle song of the evening wind. Or perhaps the reassuring gentle splashing of a little brook that quietly runs through the garden.

An experienced tea hostess will know from the sound of the water whether the correct temperature has been reached. If the water becomes too hot, she will add a little fresh water from the porcelain water jug at her side. This preserves the youthful vigour of the water. Finally, the tea hostess takes a whisk.

The shape of the whisk, called the chasen, makes it peculiarly suited to its task. The shape derives from the tea ceremonies of hundreds of years ago and has remained substantially unchanged since. The whisk is made of bamboo. There are more than 50 stages in the making of a bamboo stirring whisk. The tea hostess will now use the chasen to whisk the tea. This, too, will be done using a gentle, continuous motion, which, like all the actions and movements, follow traditional rules.

Hours of practice and years of experience are needed to be able to whisk the tea and water with grace and confidence.

This 'froth of liquid jade', as it was once described by an ancient tea master, is individually prepared for each guest, so that the hostess whisks only a relatively small quantity of tea and water for each portion.

Each guest uses both hands to receive the portion being handed to him. At the same time, he takes hold of the silk napkin, the kobukusa, underneath his tea bowl. He lifts the bowl in a gesture of thanks towards his hostess.

At the same time he bows to ask his neighbour's forgiveness for being served before him.

He then turns his bowl to a position determined by its shape and decoration and slowly begins to drink the tea.

All guests will now have enjoyed their tea and they will focus their attention on the utensils and the tea-bowl itself. Each piece is admired at length.

A bowl that at first appears somewhat coarse and unimpressive may yet be the most precious of all. It may be the work of an old master and it may have been such a particular favourite of a legendary tea-master that he himself signed it. Another bowl may not be so precious and yet it will tell its own tale.

The bowl in use today again bears the image of the crane. It was painted on to the delicate grey-blue bowl by a skilled artist who used just a few brush strokes. The quiet conversations during the tea ceremony are concerned with old masters, great artists, with cranes that migrate to warmer lands, with autumn and with the magic of the holy Mount Fuji.

those found in the small garden in front of the tea room. The hostess has gone to great lengths to see that everything is in order for her guests. There must be nothing visually intrusive, which may spoil their experience. There should be no unnecessary tastes or smells. A careful hostess will have made discrete enquiries beforehand as to the likes and dislikes of her guests. It would be quite inappropriate for her guests to be served an elaborate dish, only for her to find out later that it was not really to their taste.

After their meal, the guests may take a little walk through the garden. A crane may fly overhead, as the sun finally sets.

The Tea Hostess

The hostess will ask the guests to return to the tea room. The water in the kettle will already be singing quietly and a tea-caddy and a bowl for the water will have been carefully placed on the mats.

Then the hostess will enter, in her other role as mistress of the tea ceremony. She will be bearing a tea-bowl in both hands, together with a narrow cloth of linen and a bamboo brush. A bamboo spoon is placed across the tea bowl ready for the tea.

The hostess will put these down in their proper place, go out and return with a slop-basin, a ladle and a stand for the hot lid.

While the tea hostess adopts the correct pose on the tatami mats, the guests wait in earnest for the tea ceremony to begin. Everything follows a long-established tradition, every gesture, every movement of the hand has its place in this ancient ritual.

First of all, there is the symbolic washing ritual. First the spoon for the tea and then the tea caddy are wiped with a clean silk napkin, known as the fukusa. A bamboo ladle, which is only ever used once, is used to transfer a little hot water from the tea-kettle into the tea-bowl. The tea-bowl itself is dried, using a pure white linen cloth.

The hostess will lay this cloth over the edges of the bowl and rotate it, until it is completely dry. This ritual is one which not only symbolically cleans the tea-bowl, but the careful and considered movements help the tea hostess to relax and to create the right mood.

Cleaning the utensils in the presence of the guests not only ensures that they are spotlessly clean but also shows the guests that the hostess has concern for their welfare.

Next, the hostess places the dry bowl in the right place just in front of her and she carefully lays the folded used linen cloth on the edge of the lid of the kettle, to the side of the tea-kettle itself. She then takes the thin, curved bamboo spoon for the tea from the tea-caddy. Slowly and thoughtfully, she will open the tea-caddy. Such care is taken to ensure that the slightly conical mound of tea in the caddy is not disturbed. She will carefully take two or three spoonfuls and slowly let the tea fall into the bowl, so that another conical mound is formed, just as in the caddy. Once the last spoonful has been emptied into the bowl, the tea hostess will tap the spoon gently against the inner edge of the bowl. This makes sure that every last particle of tea ends up in the bowl and the gentle tapping sound, not too loud and not too soft, helps the guests to concentrate on the ceremony.

Fresh, clear spring water is taken from the kettle, using the ladle. The hostess will perform this task in one continuous and flowing movement. Under no circumstances should the water make any distracting bubbling sounds as the ladle is filled. Then the hostess will slowly pour about a third of the hot water from the ladle into the bowl.

The hostess will have made sure that the water does not boil. It should only just simmer. A slight draught of air over the charcoal ensures that there is an even output of heat.

The water in the kettle will simmer

undisturbed, reminding guests of the gentle song of the evening wind. Or perhaps the reassuring gentle splashing of a little brook that quietly runs through the garden.

An experienced tea hostess will know from the sound of the water whether the correct temperature has been reached. If the water becomes too hot, she will add a little fresh water from the porcelain water jug at her side. This preserves the youthful vigour of the water. Finally, the tea hostess takes a whisk.

The shape of the whisk, called the chasen, makes it peculiarly suited to its task. The shape derives from the tea ceremonies of hundreds of years ago and has remained substantially unchanged since. The whisk is made of bamboo. There are more than 50 stages in the making of a bamboo stirring whisk. The tea hostess will now use the chasen to whisk the tea. This, too, will be done using a gentle, continuous motion, which, like all the actions and movements, follow traditional rules.

Hours of practice and years of experience are needed to be able to whisk the tea and water with grace and confidence.

This 'froth of liquid jade', as it was once described by an ancient tea master, is individually prepared for each guest, so that the hostess whisks only a relatively small quantity of tea and water for each portion.

Each guest uses both hands to receive the portion being handed to him. At the same time, he takes hold of the silk napkin, the kobukusa, underneath his tea bowl. He lifts the bowl in a gesture of thanks towards his hostess.

At the same time he bows to ask his neighbour's forgiveness for being served before him.

He then turns his bowl to a position determined by its shape and decoration and slowly begins to drink the tea.

All guests will now have enjoyed their tea and they will focus their attention on the utensils and the tea-bowl itself. Each piece is admired at length.

A bowl that at first appears somewhat coarse and unimpressive may yet be the most precious of all. It may be the work of an old master and it may have been such a particular favourite of a legendary tea-master that he himself signed it. Another bowl may not be so precious and yet it will tell its own tale.

The bowl in use today again bears the image of the crane. It was painted on to the delicate grey-blue bowl by a skilled artist who used just a few brush strokes. The quiet conversations during the tea ceremony are concerned with old masters, great artists, with cranes that migrate to warmer lands, with autumn and with the magic of the holy Mount Fuji.

THE EQUIPMENT FOR THE TEA CEREMONY

Chakin: the linen cloth. It is always spotlessly white and is used to dry the tea bowl.

Chasen: the stirring whisk. It is made of bamboo and hand-crafted. There are more than 50 stages that an experienced maker has to go through to make a whisk from a single piece of bamboo. The shape of the chasen was designed hundreds of years ago and has changed little since. The best whisks come from Chasenmura, which, when translated, reads Stirring Whisk Village.

Chashaku: the spoon for the tea. It is made of bamboo and is about 20 cm/8 in long. It is slightly curved at its lower end.

Chawan: the tea-bowl. It can be simple and yet unique. It can be very beautiful and yet be very plain. It may be quite unremarkable and yet tell a two-hundred-year-old tale. In any event, it always has a special significance and is made from the very finest porcelain.

Fukusa: the small silk napkin. This is used symbolically to clean the tea caddy and the tea spoon in the guests' presence.

Furo: the charcoal-burning hearth. There should always be a slight draught, so that neither the coals nor the water become too hot.

Futaoki: a rest for the lid of the tea-kettle. The ladle, too, can be rested on this.

Hishaku: the ladle. It is made of bamboo. A new ladle is used for each tea ceremony.

Kama: the tea-kettle. It stands over the glowing charcoal and is filled with the finest fresh spring water. The water should always simmer gently and never become too hot.

Kensui: the slop-basin. This is used to hold the water that was drawn from the kettle with the ladle but was not poured into the tea-bowl.

Kobukusa: a larger silk napkin. It is laid under the tea bowl as this is handed to the guest. He takes hold of the napkin and tea bowl with both hands.

Matcha: the green tea. Fresh tea leaves are steamed, dried and ground to a fine powder in a stone mill. Green tea is rich in vitamin C. Only green tea, albeit in a number of varieties, is used in the tea ceremony.

Mizusashi: a container for cold water. It is filled with the same water as that in the tea-kettle, but this water is cold so that, should the water in the kettle become too hot, the youthful vigour of the water can be renewed with cold water.

Natsume: the tea-caddy. This is small and easy to handle. It is never filled to the brim with tea. Instead, there must be a rounded heap of tea inside it.

SEASONINGS

SEASONINGS

In Japan, the use of the correct seasonings is particularly important. For example, Japanese cuisine would be wholly incomplete without dashi or fish stock. These clear soups are used in much the same way in Japan as consommé is in Europe. The delicate aroma is used for subtly flavouring soups, vegetable dishes or sauces. By contrast with European stocks, dashi is completely fat-free.

Basic Recipe for 1 Litre/1¾ pints Fish Stock (Dashi)

One piece of kombu (dried seaweed), approximately 10 cm x 10 cm/4 in x 4 in, and 30 g/1 oz of katsuobushi (bonito flakes).

For the dashi to be well made, it is vital that the dried seaweed is dabbed with a damp cloth. Take care not to remove the layer of powdery deposits that form as the seaweed is dried. Only dirt and sand should be removed. Nor should kombu should be washed, or it will lose its flavour. To help to release the aroma, several cuts should be made in the cleaned kombu using a pair of kitchen scissors. Then place the kombu in a pan with 1 l/1¾ pints cold water. Under no circumstances should the pan be covered, as the stock might otherwise become cloudy and acquire an unpleasant flavour. Bring the water to the boil over a strong to medium heat. When the bubbles start to rise at the edge of the pan, test the kombu at its thickest point to see whether it is soft. It is at this moment that the kombu releases its full flavour into the water. Remove the kombu from the water before it starts to boil and add a bowl of cold water to halt the cooking process. Now add the bonito flakes and bring the water to the boil once more. Remove the pan from the heat and wait until the katsuobushi has sunk to the bottom of the pan.

Now strain the stock, taking care that flakes do not pass through the sieve.

If the fish stock has been made correctly, it should now be clear and without a trace of katsuobushi.

If only a small quantity of fish stock is required, instant dashi is available in powdered form or as a liquid concentrate.

Short glossary of Japanese spices and seasonings

Ao-nori: green seaweed flakes. Do not confuse ao-nori with nori. Ao-nori is available in flakes or powder. It is normally used as a spice.

Goma: black or white sesame seeds. In some recipes, sesame paste is used. It is made by toasting the sesame seeds in a dry frying-pan, stirring constantly. Remove them from the pan the moment they start to release the oil and swell up. Grind the toasted seeds to a coarse paste in a blender or food processor before passing them through a fine sieve.

Goma-abura: sesame oil. An oil with a wonderful aroma of its own. It should be used sparingly.

Hikicha: green tea ground to a powder. The fresh tea leaves are dried carefully and finely-ground. Hikicha lends a delicate fragrance and a little colour to many dishes.

Hijiki: dried, pressed seaweed. It must be thoroughly washed and left to soak for 30 minutes before use. Hijiki swells to something like 8 times its original size while soaking.

Kampyo: dried strips of gourd. The flesh of the gourd is cut into long thin strips and dried. White, evenly-shaped strips are considered the best. Kampyo has a distinctly sweetish aroma. Before use, the strips of kampyo are softened by moistening them slightly and rubbing them with salt. They are then left to soak in water for about 15 minutes and afterwards boiled in water until soft. They are mostly used in sushi and cooked dishes.

Kanten: dried red algae. They must be cleaned and soaked before use. This is not, however, necessary in the case of powdered red algae. Kanten is mainly used in the making of sweets.

Karashi: Japanese yellow mustard. Karashi is normally available in powdered form and mixed with water before use. When making mustard, use only a little mustard powder with quite hot water. Leave it to stand, covered, for about 10 minutes until the spicy aroma has had an opportunity to develop fully. If you need a substitute, use English mustard powder mixed with water.

Katsuobushi: dried bonito. After removing the scales, head, tail fins and bones, the bonito are divided into three equal parts. These are first steamed and then dried to form very hard blocks. Using a special tool, flakes are then scraped from the blocks, and these are used as the basic ingredient in fish stock (dashi). The best quality blocks are heavy, hard and shiny .

Kombu: dried seaweed. In shops you will find thicker seaweed leaves sold in a dry form. Kombu is an essential ingredient in fish stock (dashi). Before use, the seaweed, which comes covered with a thin white powdery layer, must be carefully wiped with a damp cloth. However, it must not be washed, since this powdery layer should be preserved.

Konnyaku: a transparent, gelatinous substance, processed from the tuberous roots of a vegetable called devil's tongue. Konnyaku itself has very little flavour, but it absorbs liquids and flavours readily. It is

Recipe index

ALPHABETICAL INDEX